Dr. Rob Byrd

BIBLICAL WORSHIP

Is it what
you
think?

WINEPRESS **WP** PUBLISHING

Dedication

To all the lone preachers (ministers or pastors) of small congregations throughout the world who serve unswervingly with no apparent earthly encouragement. You know what biblical worship is.

Table of Contents

Acknowledgments

T hank you, readers, for becoming a part of this study with me. I encourage you to stay with it, even through the lessons that seem to be asking for too much. Thank you Ashley Fowlkes, Michelle Byrd, and Kelli Byrd for trudging through the initial edits.

PART I: BACKGROUND

1

Introduction

"Therefore, my beloved, just as you have always obeyed me,
not only in my presence, but much more now in my absence,
work out your own salvation with fear and trembling."

(Philippians 2:12, NRSV)

Rationale

Over the last few years several topics have been hot publishing opportunities. In the early nineties several books were published on the idea of the church as a social organization and how it reflected secular culture. Another pertinent topic is that of worship.

Authors hit the idea of worship from a variety of angles, from women's role in the church (which usually translates to what women can or cannot do during the worship assembly), to how the worship service can be made more inspirational. Invariably, authors have called for some new, often controversial practice such as praise teams, projected songs, Lord's Feast rather than Lord's

Supper, lifting holy hands, kneeling, and so on to invigorate congregational worship.

While I refuse to argue in this study for or against any of these practices, I will make a single comment about them. They do not, for the most part, address what I understand to be the critical elements of worship.

In this study, you may be tempted to skip right to the "good" part where biblical worship is defined and expounded. But, if at all possible, resist the urge and stay with me. Try not to think of yourself as a reader, but as a study partner. I assure you, the end result will be much more rewarding.

Simply knowing how the book ends will not necessarily help you *become* what the book's conclusion calls for. One "light bulb" joke goes something like this: "How many psychologists does it take to change a light bulb? . . . Only one, but the light bulb has to *want* to change." Whether individual church members, leaders, or even congregations, all of us are similar to light bulbs in the hands of a psychologist. Mere knowledge is not enough. The continual improvement that God is looking for in us comes only when both the knowledge and the motivation to change are present (Matthew 7:24, James 1:22, etc.). Providing only the facts without attempting to motivate change is an exercise in futility. So, even though it may seem like a "long-cut" (as my young son, Reuben, says), the study is laid out with the hope that we can achieve the greatest long-term growth.

Overview of the Study

What follows is an overview of how our study will develop. If you are using this as a quarterly Bible class or small group study, you will surely want to spend two weeks in Chapter Four. And after Chapter Seven, you will want to spend a week looking at Appendix B, Non-Participant Observation of the Worship Hour. Depending on the response of others in the class, you may find yourself spending two quarters on the material.

Part One, including this section, supplies the background information necessary to make the book a useful tool for the interested Christian. Because this writing is fundamentally a word study, some things must be said about the importance of words and word usage. Without this preliminary impetus for the correct use of key words, the study will not have real meaning or validity for application.

Similarly, unless we can argue that our current understanding is imperfect, or at least not uniquely correct, it would not be enough to show there is a more logical or appropriate approach to understanding worship. Just as knowledge has a necessary partner—motivation—so a new, and possibly more appropriate approach to worship requires an accompanying belief in continuous improvement rather than the cliched belief that "if it's been good enough for the last fifty years, it's good enough now." Einstein did not claim that classical mechanics were nonsense. He simply developed a theory to explain the physical world that held up over a broader range of situations. If there is an approach to worship that seems to make more biblical sense, don't we have an obligation to at least investigate the approach, and maybe even to attempt its implementation?

After we explore the concept of continuous improvement, we can begin the word study in Part Two. Scripture references of the word *worship* will be explicitly discussed and categorized in an attempt to determine the meanings of the translation to English. Next, we will briefly look at the specific Greek words used for *worship* and discuss the relationship the various words have to each other. After completing the *worship* word study, we will investigate how the word *together* is used (or not used) in conjunction with worship. The results may be surprising.

In Part Three we will discuss some immediate and long-term implications of biblical worship. The fourth and final part will provide closure and offer some ideas for those wishing to implement biblical worship. Appendix A contains a set of discussion and application questions. Not using these questions in your study will significantly reduce its effectiveness since many integral points of the study will mean more when study participants discover them independently. The second appendix is an account of what an outsider might observe when going to a typical "worship service." The account is painstakingly accurate, as I recorded it while posing as a non-participant observer of a worship hour. The third appendix contains a word study of the word *church*, which is integral to the understanding and perception of worship. Many disagreements on the topic of worship could be eliminated if we had a better understanding of what the Bible meant when it said *church*. The fourth appendix expounds on some possibilities as to where we may have developed some of our current practices of religion.

Why This Approach?

As a computer science teacher, my primary purpose is not to impart knowledge, but to assist in student learning. Computer programming is basically complex problem solving. The expertise of writing software programs cannot be successfully acquired simply by taking notes from a professor, but by engaging in the problem-solving process. While most of the knowledge required to write a real-world computer program comes not from computer science, but from the discipline that the software application will be used in (such as banking, chemistry, or astrophysics), there is still a substantial amount of knowledge required in the process of designing and writing the code.

So it is with understanding biblical worship. I could "lecture" in this book, and be very humorous and wordy. However, that would not necessarily facilitate learning. By choice, I have determined to do what I can to increase learning by providing the tools you need to complete the study and let you make your own conclusions.

Ultimately, you are responsible for your worship. Even if I were an ordained prophet of God, you, yourself would be responsible for your understanding of worship and how you applied it. We have a chilling illustration of this point in the story of the two prophets in 1 Kings 13.

As you recall, there was a man of God who was given some specific travel instructions by God in addition to the prophetic message he was to deliver. A second prophet of God deceitfully persuaded the first man of God into disobeying God's original travel instructions. The lying prophet then correctly prophesied that the first man of God would die because he listened to the lie. To find out the gruesome way he died, read it for yourself.

The application of the story of the two prophets is that, even if I were an inspired prophet of God and were lying to trick you into believing some wild, non-biblical message, you would also be responsible for following the error. You would have the same personal responsibility even if the message were coming from your trusted preacher or pastor.

I hope you are beginning to understand what I am talking about with my teaching method. If you are not considering this book a biblical study, then you will not be learning what I intend for this book to teach you. I am providing a process for the study, but the real knowledge will come from you assertively searching the Scriptures (and your heart) to understand more about the topic.

A secondary purpose for this book is to learn to be more responsible for our spiritual growth rather than to depend on church leaders or renowned authors to feed us. Today's culture has lulled us into thinking that if we hire an expert, we are no longer accountable.

2

Words Have Meaning

"[O]n the last day the word that I have spoken will serve as judge."

(John 12:48b, NRSV)

Careless Conversation Content Causes Confusing Communication

Inappropriate use of words may cause our hearers to understand something different than what we mean to convey. Notice, I didn't use the word *misunderstand* because that might have put the blame on the receiving end of the communication. Just as often, the cause of misunderstanding is with the sender, for reasons we will now discuss.

Different types of inappropriate word usage may include using vague words, the extensive use of superlatives, or talking in faddy jargon. Allow me to give short examples of each.

Some vague or indefinite words are *thing, that, this,* and *there*. Admittedly, I have been known to miscommunicate by saying something like, "Hand me that Phillips screw driver right there." Pointing with my eyes, when I was on the top step of a ladder, I then wondered why my helper (usually a son or daughter) couldn't find it. Never mind the fact that they didn't even know what a Phillips screwdriver was.

Another way to miscommunicate is through the extensive use of superlatives. Overusing these superlatives tends to desensitize our thinking so that, when a superlative *is* appropriate, there is no remaining way to incite the necessary attention, except maybe verbal or physical violence. Examples of overused superlatives are *all, always, never, best, worst, very, really*, and even *love*. Just as writing e-mail messages in capital letters connotes SHOUTING, so the overuse of superlatives is an inappropriate use of words and ultimately detracts from the understanding of the message.

Most generations seem to have their distinctive faddy jargon. In the sixties, anything we liked was either hot, cool, groovy, or neat. Talk about today's jargon; like duh, well, like it has like a few possibly extra things that like maybe we, "furell" [for real] dude, don't really like need, "noamsain" [know what I am saying]? And you already know the response I get when calling attention to the jargon . . . . What-ever! . . . By the way, my three teenage daughters say I'm getting pretty good at it. I'm not suggesting we should punish those who talk like this, as we should become all things to all men, especially our own children. However, as unintentional as generational or other jargon may be, as with the use of superlatives, it is an inappropriate use of words when used in general conversation, and ultimately detracts from the understanding of the message. I am not a sociologist, but it may be that this form of miscommunication may not only be a form of rebellion by the younger generation, but also a form of alienation of the older generation who has genuine difficulty in keeping pace with the fluid vocabulary of today.

I will only briefly mention the concept of purposely changing the meaning, as some do, in an attempt to coerce others toward a different way of thinking or acting. Consider the psychology of advertising. By redefining for us what beauty, happiness, and comfort are, the advertisers sometimes talk us into buying things that we neither want, need, nor can afford.

It is possible for this miscommunication to occur even within the church. In fact, when we continuously use inappropriate words, we can even begin to change our understanding of the truth.

Removing inappropriate words that cause communication barriers obviously takes planning, effort, and practice. It also requires knowledge of the subject we are trying to communicate, a relationship with the other party, and an attitude of trying to understand, as well as wanting to be understood. Stephen Covey (Covey 1989) considered trying to understand others first, one of the seven habits of highly effective people. Whether leaders in the church or not, effective communication with other Christians is critical to the success and health of the congregation.

Call Bible Things by Bible Names

One subset of the evangelical movement grew out of what was known as the Restoration Movement. That heritage brings with it mottoes like "We are Christians only, but not the only Christians," "Speak where the Bible speaks and keep silent where the Bible is silent," "Call Bible things by Bible names," "In faith unity; in opinions liberty; in all things love," etc.

Through their lyrics, the a capella singing group, AVB (A Capella Vocal Band), has educated much of the brotherhood that "you can't go to church 'cause the church is you." In the *mind* of most Christians this concept is well understood. Our speech betrays us, not only by telling others incorrectly that the church is a building rather than an assembly of God's people, but by eventually changing our way of thinking. Eventually, we tend to emphasize the importance of the building over the importance of our brothers and sisters in Christ.

Those who believe in baptism as immersion only would not agree that we have the freedom to interpret baptism in whatever way we like, such as sprinkling, pouring, or even merely a symbolic act. They would argue that baptism means complete immersion as was done in the first century. Yet some Christians have argued regarding other pertinent topics, including the definition of worship, saying, "You have your idea about what it means, and I have my idea. It means whatever you want it to mean for you." Paul's discussion on acceptance and tolerance in Romans 14 and 15 notwithstanding, it seems that, at some point, Christians should be concerned about finding out what a concept really means rather than adopting the culturally current existential philosophy: "Do what's right for you."

Calling Bible things by Bible names requires that we know the Bible, just as the motto "speak where Bible speaks and be silent where it is silent" requires scriptural knowledge. In addition to knowledge, it is good to discuss with others exactly what we mean when we are referring to an activity or a concept.

If biblical worship means one thing and we do something else and call it worship, how can we honestly say that we are calling Bible things by Bible names, or that we follow the Bible only? We will discuss this in more detail in the following chapters, but here, the two main points are: 1) improperly naming concepts and events can lead, and has led, people astray in their thinking; and 2) it is hypocritical to say we know the truth if we don't also speak (much less act) the truth.

Greek Language Is Very Specific

The specific words used in the biblical writings can be trusted not only because of divine inspiration (as if that weren't enough), but also because of the common language used during the time when the New Testament was written. Regarding the *koine* Greek dialect, Dr. F. W. Mattox (Mattox 1961, 29) claimed, "There is no language known to man that could be better used to convey a divine message . . . The language itself possesses tenses and moods that enable an exactness of expression not possible in English." So there was definitely a capability within the language to choose words that had a particular meaning. We must trust that with the Spirit's help and such a definitive language, the words chosen had the exact intended meaning.

Logical Interpretation of Words (from Base Words) has Some Merit

My children's high school has in its curriculum a text called Classical Roots. The idea is that by learning the meaning and origin of base words, prefixes, and suffixes, students will not only greatly increase their vocabulary, but will also be able to speak and write using words that are most appropriate. For the English language, the words usually originate from either Latin or Greek. I sometimes use this form of analysis when teaching college students, and I never cease to be amazed at the number of students who haven't looked at language in this manner before.

One familiar example of this concept would be the *television*. Tele—means far, and—vision deals with getting a look at something. So a *television* is a device that allows one to get a look at something far away. A computer *monitor*, on the other hand, is a device that allows its user to *monitor* the results of the processing unit, and it doesn't necessarily allow one to get a look at something far away. Of course, if one has a *modem*, which is a device that *modulates* and *demodulates* signals sent over a *telephone* (tele—far, phono—sound or voice), and if it is connected to the *Internet* (inter—between or among, net—a connected system of string or wire), a simple computer *monitor* could be *transformed* [look this one up yourself] into a *television* of sorts.

Okay, that was just for fun, but here is another one to aim us back toward our Greek word study on worship. *Hippopotamus* comes from the Greek words *hippos* (for horse) and *potamos* (for river). Knowing the base words, we can perceive more meaning from the compound word than if we simply had to memorize the long word, hippopotamus, as a certain kind of animal found in Africa.

While the commonly recognized usage of some words such as *ecstatic* may not seem to fit this pattern, a closer look brings better results—and a better understanding of the word. Most think of ecstatic as being really excited or maybe even "jumping for joy." I have heard some in the older generation say, "I was so happy I was beside myself." A second definition of the word ecstasy actually refers to the emotional or religious frenzy or trance that some elude to as an out-of-body experience. This is more than coincidentally reminiscent of being beside oneself. The Greek for ecstasy is *ekstasis* which means literally "standing outside oneself." As adults, maybe we would do well to better analyze words in an attempt to more appropriately convey or gather their intended meanings.

Let me say again that while these introductory chapters may not seem important now, they are laying an important logical foundation. When a word from the Bible is used in a certain way, it is close-minded to dismiss its intended use and define it according to what our previous understanding, or practice, of that word may have been. Please use these introductory principles as a background for how you accept and apply the results of this study.

3

Continuous Improvement

"For if you possess these qualities in increasing measure, they will keep you from being ineffective and unproductive in your knowledge of our Lord Jesus Christ."

(2 Peter 1:8)

"But grow in the grace and knowledge of our Lord and Savior Jesus Christ."

(2 Peter 3:18)

Quality Perspective

Process analysis and systems thinking are basic principles of quality management in industry. Right along with these basic elements is the concept of continuous improvement. American industry has adopted the Japanese term for continuous improvement, *kaizen*. The idea is that small incremental change is where the ultimate advantage in competition will be found. Re-engineering, or large, drastic change, is also necessary at times. Another way to think about these two forms of change are as evolution (small incremental change) and revolution (drastic change or re-engineering).

Within the church now, as in the first century, both forms of change are sometimes necessary. I won't take the time to expound on this, other than to say that just as the many small earth tremors due to the pressure built up along a fault line in the earth's crust may prevent the occurrence of a major earthquake, so, too, many small changes in a congregation or movement may prevent the necessity of a revolution or revolt. Think about it.

Biblical Roots of Change for Improvement

In many biblical passages God calls for or encourages change for improvement. Some admonitions are for incremental changes, while others are for complete re-engineering. The apostle Peter, in his second letter, encourages us to build Christian virtues on the foundation of our basic faith in Christ (2 Peter 1:3–10). He then adds that we should be continually improving in these areas. The New International Version uses the phrase "increasing measure." Romans 12:2 says that we are to be transformed from within. Ephesians 4:22–24 explains how we are to be renewed. In Christ, we are being transformed with "ever increasing glory" (2 Corinthians 3:18).

The concept of newness is also common in biblical teachings and is characteristic of radical or revolutionary change. Paul stated that "If anyone is in Christ, there is a new creation: everything old has passed away; see, everything has become new" (2 Corinthians 5:17, NRSV). Think about the entire earthly life of Christ. From his conversation with Nicodemus about rebirth (John 3) to the Sermon on the Mount (Matthew 5 - 7), Christ was all about calling us to change for the better—both through revolutionary and evolutionary improvement.

If we are not willing to accept the challenge and command given to us by God to change, and to continuously improve as we learn more about his principles and guidelines for us, then we are like the man James mentioned, who looks in the mirror and then immediately forgets what he looks like once he turns away (James 1:22–25), or, like the philosophers on Mars Hill who loved learning, but didn't necessarily want to change or apply the learning (Acts 17:18–32).

Tradition and Leave Well Enough Alone

As previously mentioned, one motto within the restoration movement has been to speak where the Bible speaks and to be silent where the Bible is silent. I should now reemphasize a critical point to this motto. We must *know* what the Bible says before we can speak or be silent appropriately. Today we sometimes talk as if we knew the Bible when we only know recent tradition. Paul warned, in Colossians 2:8, not to be taken captive by ideas that are based on human tradition. The only way we can be sure about what true doctrines are is to know the Bible ourselves. We will then change our question from what do "we believe" about such and such to what does the "Bible say" about it.

While teaching in a Sunday night auditorium session on the topic of traditions, I once mentioned that many practices such as the use of King James Version, the use of songbooks, and even the pews we were sitting on were nothing more than tradition. One man immediately responded with, "Just a minute, pews are scriptural," implying they were scripturally required. This raised my curiosity so I asked how. He came back with three "scriptural" reasons why pews were required. "Well, first, it says 'they sat around the table.' Do you think they were sitting on the floor? Two, 'Jesus went up on a mountainside and sat down.' Do you think he sat on the ground? And three, haven't you seen *the picture*?" (his emphasis). I could only presume he was referring to one of the Renaissance painter's impression of the Last Supper. That's when I knew I had taken the class far enough for one night.

By the way, if you don't know the answers to his questioning rebuttals, they are: 1) Yes, they probably did sit on the floor, or at most a backrest or cushion, reclining on their left side, since this was the Jewish custom; 2) Yes, he probably sat on the ground or a convenient rock, as church campfire log benches were not common in first century deserts; and 3) Excuse me, but Christ lived about 1,500 years before the paintings were produced, and we really don't want to start considering this Renaissance painting authoritative or we would also be obligated to accept other paintings as authoritative. Thankfully, being as young and cynical as I was, I didn't think of these responses until after I got home that night.

Restoration Movement

Flavel Yeakley, a researcher in church growth (Yeakley 1979, 121), asserted that one of the reasons for the church's numerical decline was that congregations "do not want to have anyone challenge them to an ever-increasing level of Christianity." While I am admittedly a restorationist, I will also just as freely admit that I am not an expert in restoration history. It does seem, however, that one of the main tenets of the early restoration movement was that of open learning and challenging each other to continually throw off the worldly aspects of the church organization and to continually go back to the simple truths found in God's Word.

Early restorationists, Alexander Campbell and Barton W. Stone, claimed unity in Christ and Christian principles by ending their allegiance to the other denominations, yet fellowshipped with Christians from several denominations. They apparently did this not because they wanted to "trick" them into being converted, but because they had a genuine spirit of love and acceptance, realizing that God was not a respecter of persons. Foremost in their minds was the idea that they should continually strive to improve their Christian theology and practice.

Restorationists from then until now have discussed restoration using terms such as non-sectarianism and un-denominationalism. These terms are also key to the concept of worship, although I will not be using them directly. While I personally consider this current study to cover a specific aspect within the realm of restoration, the scope of general restoration is too large to discuss here, and I must yield to those whose life work has been studying and publishing about the restoration movement. For those interested in modern restoration, let me recommend any or all of the books written by Monroe Hawley, a renowned restoration-ist, author, and publisher (Hawley 1976, 1981, 1985, and 1992).

Social-Spiritual Evolution of the Church

As I mentioned earlier, during the early 1990s several books were published explaining how the church should not function as a worldly modern cultural organization, but should be the church as Christ founded it and intended it to be. One example of another focus in publications and lectureships has recently been on the "worship service" and how to make it more inspiring. The emphasis has generally still been on what the participants do during the worship hour, and, to a large degree, how to transform observers into participants.

While these approaches are not wrong, it can readily be argued that they will not be completely accepted, or at least not be effective, as long as the traditional mindset of worship exists. I would here like to applaud the writers of the works mentioned only generally here and restate that they have been good for the brotherhood, not only by in-spiring much thought on the topic of worship, but also by showing that the traditional structure of worship was just that—tradition, not law. Much good has come from them. Most recently, the Lord's Supper has been reinvestigated as a possible area of improvement.

In fact, as the logical conclusions of those books are reached, they hopefully lead disciples to the same place that my experiences and study have taken me. It is in the same spirit of those writers that we must forge on in the continual restoration of the Lord's church.

PART II: WORSHIP VERSUS FELLOWSHIP

Typically, the center of what most consider the "worship service" is the solemn occasion identified as the Lord's Supper or the Communion Service. The traditional mindset is for utmost quiet to be observed—no talking, no playing, and positively no singing. Since the congregation appears to go into a deeper mode of worship during the Lord's Supper, one might assume this to be the most sacred time of the worship service. I remember as a second grader hearing my aunt tell me that we should be quieter during the Lord's Supper than during a prayer. And I already knew to be quieter than a mouse during prayers. Paradoxically, she was telling me this during the Lord's Supper.

Would my aunt have felt different knowing that the traditional word for Lord's Supper is Eucharist, which means thanksgiving? She might have been less concerned about telling me to be quiet and used the opportunity to express the joy we as Christians have in being redeemed by the blood of the Lamb and the fellowship we have with a risen Savior and his people.

In the account of the last supper eaten by Jesus and his disciples, John recorded a conversation that was not about the bread or fruit of the vine. It involved Peter and John talking across the table about some topic irrelevant to the Lord's Supper. I can imagine the almost gossipy tone that Peter used. "Hey, psst, John. Find out who this betrayer is going to be . . . Tell me . . . What'd he say?" (Very loose paraphrase of John 13:24). It seems as if, though in the presence of God, the disciples were more interested in fellowshipping with each other than in recognizing the occasion as solemn and quiet. Were they more concerned about each other than remembering how the death angel passed over their forefathers' homes in Egypt?

In the same sense, with the rest of the worship hour, what I had been told and had seen all my life seemed to misrepresent what I read in Scripture. I realized it was time to study worship for myself. I have specifically mentioned the Lord's Supper as an activity where we have focused so intently on "correct worship" that we may have missed the boat on fellowshipping with Jesus and his disciples. It seems that we know 1 Corinthians 11 tells us to examine ourselves, but somehow we miss that what we are to be examining is how much we are thinking about others during this time. Rather than examining ourselves to keep "recognizing the body" (1 Corinthians 11:29), we tend to examine ourselves to see that we are sinless (never gonna happen) or solemn enough.

In this word study on worship, we'll begin by finding, through the use of a complete concordance, all the references to that word in the Bible. I happened to have used the NIV translation. Next, we will correlate each reference with a Greek translation to determine the original word used.

Don't think that you are going to need a degree in Bible languages to get through this study—it may be from out of this world, but it is not rocket science. Every earnest disciple of Christ should have access to a complete concordance. And you can look up the Greek words in a *Strong's Concordance* or a Greek lexicon. Each word in *Strong's Concordance* has a reference number beginning with either a G or an H. G stands for Greek word and H stands for Hebrew word. All the words we look up will be referenced beginning with a G.

To complete the study, we will then correlate, back to the English translation, all references to each of the Greek words used for worship. So some of the references may not actually say worship, but in those cases, the original Greek word could also have been translated into worship. Different translations may have greater or fewer instances, because the Bible translators thought the context indicated a different word to be more meaningful. Let me say here that I am in no way intending to second guess the words chosen for any Bible translation. I fully trust the committees of translators to have used the most appropriate word.

Similarly, in the study of the word *together*, I found all the references to the word and then discarded those that seemed to me to be irrelevant. It may be that a couple references relevant from your viewpoint are omitted. That's another reason why I encourage you to actually do the study yourself and not rely on me. But I did not purposely leave out any references just to make my point. When I originally completed this study, I had no point to make other than to see what God's Word had to say to me about worship and being together. Let me reemphasize here: I have done the study, but don't take my word for it; actually do the study yourself.

4

Worship Word Study

"I am amply supplied, now that I have received from Epaphroditus the gifts you sent. They are a fragrant offering, an acceptable sacrifice, pleasing to God."

(Philippians 4:18)

L isted below are the primary references to the words translated "to worship." My suggestion for you is to: 1) Read the references; 2) look at the original Greek definitions that follow the references; 3) read the rest of the section on worship; and 4) use your Bible to reread the references in their full context. Once you have completed the word study, consider the Discussion/Application Questions in Appendix A.

The parenthetical phrases before each scripture are an attempt to both summarize the passage and tell what kind of worship the original Greek words meant. The first set of verses contain Greek words for the "bow down" type of worship. The second set lists verses in which the original

Greek words meaning "to serve" have been translated into worship. Don't worry about the specifics of the word definitions now. We will look at the definitions in detail after reading the primary passages on worship.

Bow Down Type of Worship

(The Magi came to pay homage to Jesus.)

"We saw his star in the east and have come to worship [bow down] him." (Matthew 2:2)

(Herod said he wanted to pay homage [bow down worship] to Jesus also.)

"As soon as you find him, report to me, so that I too may go and worship him." (Matthew 2:8)

(Jesus told Satan to worship [bow down] and serve [worship] only God.)

"Jesus said to him, 'Away from me, Satan! For it is written: "Worship the Lord your God, and serve him only."'" (Matthew 4:10) (Also in Luke 4:8.)

(Soldiers mocked Jesus by getting on their knees and paying homage [bow down worship] to him.)

"Again and again they struck him on the head with a staff and spit on him. Falling on their knees, they paid homage to him." (Mark 15:19)

(Worship [bow down] was not in a certain place, but in spirit and truth.)

"Our fathers worshiped on this mountain, but you Jews claim that the place where we must worship is in Jerusalem." Jesus declared, "Believe me, woman, a time is coming when you will worship the Father neither on this mountain nor in Jerusalem. You Samaritans worship what you do not know; we worship what we do know, for salvation is from the Jews. Yet a time is coming and has now come when the true worshipers will worship the Father in spirit and truth, for they are the kind of worshipers the Father seeks." (John 4:20–23)

(Gentiles went to worship [bow down] at a Jewish feast. See Colossians 2:13 - 17 for more insight.)

"Now there were some Greeks among those who went up to worship at the Feast." (John 12:20)

(The Israelites had false gods in their homes that they worshiped [bow down].)

"You have lifted up the shrine of Molech and the star of your god Rephan, the idols you made to worship. Therefore I will send you into exile beyond Babylon." (Acts 7:43)

(The Eunuch had gone to Jerusalem to worship [bow-down].)

"So he started out, and on his way he met an Ethiopian eunuch, an important official in charge of all the treasury of Candace, queen of the Ethiopians. This man had gone to Jerusalem to worship." (Acts 8:27)

(Paul went to Jerusalem to worship [bow down]. Offering sacrifices was his option since he was also a Jew.)

"You can easily verify that no more than twelve days ago I went up to Jerusalem to worship." (Acts 24:11)

(A single unbeliever may worship [bow down] among a fellowship of believers who are edifying each other.)

"But if an unbeliever or someone who does not understand comes in while everybody is prophesying, he will be convinced by all that he is a sinner and will be judged by all, and the secrets of his heart will be laid bare. So he will fall down and worship God, exclaiming, 'God is really among you!'" (1 Corinthians 14:24, 25)

(Even the angels worship him [bow down].)

"Let all God's angels worship him." (Hebrews 1:6)

(All nations will worship [bow down] God.)

"All nations will come and worship before you, for your righteous acts have been revealed." (Revelation 15:4)

Service Type of Worship

(Paul testified that he worshiped [serve] God.)

"However, I admit that I worship the God of our fathers as a follower of the Way, which they call a sect. I believe everything that agrees with the Law and that is written in the Prophets." (Acts 24:14)

(Ministering, serving, giving up of one's self [daily, as opposed to Sunday mornings] is what Paul was calling worship.)

"Therefore, I urge you, brothers, in view of God's mercy, to offer your bodies as living sacrifices, holy and pleasing to God—this is your spiritual act of worship." (Romans 12:1)

(We worship [serve] by the Spirit of God.)

"For it is we who are the circumcision, we who worship by the Spirit of God." (Philippians 3:3)

(Context goes from Hebrews chapter 9:1 to chapter 12:29 comparing the conditions of the Old Covenant to the new form of worship [serve] involving faith *and* action.)

"Now the first covenant had regulations for worship and also an earthly sanctuary." (Hebrews 9:1)

"Therefore, since we are receiving a kingdom that cannot be shaken, let us be thankful, and so worship God acceptably with reverence and awe, for our 'God is a consuming fire.'" (Hebrews 12:28,29)

Other Words for Worship

(Regulated, systematic, Old Law, Jewish tradition worship [*ethelothrayskia*: self-made religion], cannot change lives.)

"Such regulations indeed have an appearance of wisdom, with their self imposed worship, their false humility, and their harsh treatment of the body, but they lack any value in restraining sensual indulgence." (Colossians 2:23)

(If one professes to be a worshiper of God [*theosebeia*, from *sebw-* revers God] they will be dressed in a life of good deeds [see Romans 12:1], not fancy clothes.)

"I also want women to dress modestly, with decency and propriety, not with braided hair or gold or pearls or expensive clothes, but with good deeds, appropriate for women who profess to worship God." (1 Timothy 2:9,10)

(Jews accused Paul of teaching people to worship [*sebw-* to *revere* God] God in a wrong manner.)

"This man," they charged, "is persuading the people to worship God in ways contrary to the law." (Acts 18:13)

(Worship [*sebw*-to revere God] is considered vain when we act like or think we are worshiping, but we're really not. *Sebw* doesn't have to be used in the negative sense.)

> "These people honor me with their lips, but their hearts are far from me. They worship me in vain; their teachings are but rules taught by men." (Matthew 15:8,9) (Also in Mark 7:7.)

(Paul called together those that feared [*phobew*-to respect, fear, or be afraid of, terrified] God so he could talk to them.)

> "Standing up, Paul motioned with his hand and said: 'Men of Israel and you Gentiles who worship God, listen to me!'" (Acts 13:16)

(During the transfiguration the disciples fell in front of Jesus terrified [*phobew*-to respect, fear, or be afraid of, terrified].)

> "When the disciples heard this, they fell facedown to the ground, terrified." (Matthew 17: 6 NIV)

5

What Does the Bible Mean When It Says Worship?

"But go and learn what this means: 'I desire mercy, not sacrifice.' For I have not come to call the righteous, but sinners."
(Matthew 9:13)

Congratulations! The most tedious part of this study is over. Let's now consider what all those references mean. The following bold-faced Greek words are those translated into worship in the New Testament. As mentioned earlier, the *Strong's* reference numbers (Gnnnn, where each n is a numeric digit) are used as index words contained in the original manuscripts. The G prefix signifies a Greek word while an H prefix is for a Hebrew word (none of which are used in this study). In this chapter, definitions were taken from either *Strong's Dictionary* or the *NAS Concordance Dictionary*.

Greek Definitions

The word *proskunew* means to bow down to, with the idea of lying down and kissing the feet of the one who is worshiped. The first part of the word is from prostrate, or to lie down flat, and the second part of the word is from to kiss. The next two Greek words *latreuw* and *latreia* mean service or to serve. *Sebw* is seldom used and, in its positive context, refers to a God-fearing person or a God-fearing life. *Phobew* is used quite often as a word for afraid or terrified, but is rarely (or never, depending on the Bible version) translated as worship. Here are all the terms with their complete definitions:

proskunew [G4352], from G4314 and *kune* (to kiss); to do reverence to: could be translated as: bow down, bow down before, bowed down, bowed down before, bowing before, bowing down, prostrated himself before, worship, worshiped, worshipers, worships. *Proskunew* is used about seventy-one times in The New Testament. About twenty-seven of those times it is translated as worship.

latreuw [G3000], from *latris* (a hired servant); to serve: could be translated as: offer service, serve, served, serving, worship, worshiper, worshipers. *latreia* [G2999], from G3000; service: could be translated as: divine worship, service, service of worship. *Latreuw* and *latreia* are used about thirty times in The New Testament. About half of those times it is translated as worship and half as serve.

sebw [G4576], to worship: could be translated as: devout, God fearing, worship, worshiper. *Sebw* is used about ten times in the New Testament, and is usually translated as God-fearer or worshiper.

phobew [G5399], from G5401; to put to flight, to terrify, frighten:—could be translated as: afraid, am afraid, fear, feared, fearful, fearing, fears, filled with awe, frightened, have fear, or respect. *Phobew* is used about ninety-eight times used about in the New Testament. About half of those cases refer to being afraid of something other than God or angels. The remaining references describe fearing God or angels. In these cases, the angel or Jesus usually says "Do not be afraid." In the New American Standard translation, *phobew* is never translated as worship. In the New International Version, it is translated as worship only once.

The Worship Continuum

After looking at the words for "worship" and the references for "together," we will continue the study (as all studies should) with implications and applications. In preparation for those sections, it may be helpful to put the terms for worship in a continuum from the fear type of worship to service type of worship. Don't think I am trying to suggest that these words were specifically designed by God or the Greeks to be compared on a single worship dimension. I simply developed these ordered classifications (sometimes collectively called a rubric) to present a relationship between the words.

Phobew, sometimes translated as terrified or frightened can be defined as the immediate, Judgment Day type fear. Often, when this word is used in conjunction with angel appearances or the transfiguration, the angels, and even the Lord Jesus himself, generally say, "Do not be afraid." God may not desire for us to regularly have this type of fear within us. Rather, this is the kind of fear, according to 1 John 4:18, that people have when they expect punishment, and the kind of fear that perfect love will drive out. When *phobew* is referring to people being terrified or afraid of God, the situation is urgent, acute, critical, short-lived, and superlative. It also seems to generally convey a reaction rather than a response. Today, this may happen at the time of conversion or at some S.E.E. (significant emotional event) such as a near-death experience, etc.

Phobew may be similar to the kind of reverence I remember giving the Air Force security police on one occasion when we were on nuclear alert during the Cold War. On that memorable morning, one member of our B-52 bomber crew forgot he was without his security badge. As we were all going out to the plane for our morning preflight check, the security police noticed the badge was missing. At once there was an M-16 rifle pointed at us as I heard the police firmly ordering, "Get down to the ground!" We were commanded to lie face-down on the concrete (in below zero degree Fahrenheit temperatures) until he had radioed to the command post the badge number of each of the five badge-carrying crew members and vouched the identity of the remaining badgeless crew member, who was now going to eat crow for at least the rest of the day. I then realized why they called us crew dogs. I also then knew acute fear—not

because I was in the presence of the power or majesty of
the security police, but because I sensed the immediate
threat of an eighteen year old (or anyone, for that matter)
pointing a loaded rifle at my body.

Proskunew is next in the continuum and connotes a falling down and praising God for what he has done. Picture
those being healed by Jesus who then praise and thank him
by falling to their knees in worship. We are to worship in
this form, but this kind of worship is an individual response
that one may not be able to simply turn on and off at some
predetermined worship hour.

Proskunew worship might occur spontaneously during our morning Bible reading when tears suddenly start
flowing as we realize (again) how awesome our God is and
who fights our battles for us. I sometimes imagine how
Hezekiah's army must have felt after seeing all those dead
bodies—185,000 men in the Assyrian army—the morning
after the angel of the Lord was sent in answer to Hezekiah's
prayer (2 Kings 19:35; one of my favorite verses). We see
God's unfailing love again as we recognize another sin in our
lives and realize that he has the power and mercy to forgive
even us. If *phobew* is acute and reactive then *proskunew*
could be a spontaneous acknowledgment of God that lasts
longer and occurs more frequently than *phobew*.

Six years ago, God gave my family and me the property
on which we now live. It is known to our church family as
"Byrd Mountain." I often ride on our dilapidated tractor or
walk along the wooded driveway that was originally a log-
ging trail. During those times, I realize again how beautiful
the autumn leaves are and how God has given this dream to
me simply because I asked him to. Unable to hold back the

tears, I can't begin to express the thankfulness and appreciation I feel for the gifts that he lavishes upon me. I praise his name for his power and lovingkindness (Jeremiah 31:3). I consider this *proskunew* worship.

Sebw (*or sebomai*, in some lexicons) and its derivative *theosebeia* may fall next in the list as a general revering of God or showing reverence to God. From six of the ten biblical contexts, it sounds less reactive and indicates more of a life decision rather than an explicit act of worshiping. Of the four references where the word worship is actually used, two are in the Gospels where Jesus quoted Isaiah saying, "They worship me in vain . . ." (Matthew 15:9; Mark 7:7). One of the remaining two is when the Jews are referring to Paul teaching others to worship God incorrectly (Acts 18:13). The other is in reference to worshiping a false goddess, Artemis (Acts 19:27). If it weren't for the negative connotations of this word, I would have said *sebw* may be the best word to describe our "worship hour" . . . . Hmmm. (This is not a symbol for a *Strong's Concordance* catalog number. That would be Hnnnn. Hmmm means "Hmmm was that an epiphany or should I erase these references from my manuscript?") Maybe we really should think seriously about the "worship hour."

Just as a parenthetical thought, it is interesting to note that *epiphany* not only means a moment of sudden and great revelation as I was lightheartedly asserting, but, when capitalized, also refers to the great revelation of Christ to the Magi. Here's what the *Corel Dictionary* says about the word: epiphany >noun (pl. epiphanies) 1 (Epiphany) the manifestation of Christ to the Magi (Gospel of Matthew, chapter 2). 2 (Epiphany) the festival commemorating this, on 6 January. 3 a moment of sudden and great revelation. ORIGIN from Greek *epiphainein* "reveal."

The last word on our continuum is *latreuw* (and its alternate form, *latreia*), which is positively a proactive rather than reactive response to what the Lord has done for us. It involves, or should involve, every action we do throughout the day, every day of our born-again lives. As Romans Chapter twelve verses one and two so aptly explain, after understanding how much mercy God has for us, the only reasonable or logical response we can have is to spend the rest of our lives serving him with our entire body.

For those of you who are biblical language experts, let me explain that for at least a couple reasons I have chosen not to differentiate noun, verb, adjective, or even tense for this study. First of all, it would probably scare half the readers away, and that is definitely not the main intent of this study. Although it is scripturally and logically based, it is hopefully clear enough for everyone to read. Secondly, as you probably already are aware, depending on the translation, a noun or adjective in the original may be reworded as a pronoun or a verb in the English text. This is especially true in the NIV where the focus is on understanding the meaning of the context and not translating word for word as some other translations do.

The *latreuw* form of worship is neither acute nor spontaneous, but rather quite decisive in nature. We take on the form of a slave, a willing—even joyful—one. Whether we like the task or not, we gladly do it because we are constantly remembering what God has already done for us. We continually and eagerly anticipate the final fulfillment of his promise of eternal life, the promised rest, no matter how hard the present work seems or how "overqualified" we think we may be for an act of service. This is how we *truly* worship God while in this physical body. Even after we die and are clothed with a new heavenly body, we will continue the *proskunew* worship—bowing down with the angels and praising him for eternity.

Here is another example of what might be considered *latreuw* worship. A widow neighbor and her severely physically challenged daughter had a room that didn't seem to be heating properly. Having recently finished installing my own HVAC (heating, venting, and air conditioning) for the house we built on Byrd Mountain, I felt obligated to at least offer to look at it for her.

I assumed the problem would be something with a quick fix, such as duct tape coming loose around the flexible vent hose causing the hot air to escape before reaching the vent register. That was *not* the case. When I got into the crawlspace—which smelled worse than any sewer I had ever broken into—I found that a 'possum had made its home in the duct before getting stuck and dying. No wonder it stunk so bad. Dead opossum, infested 'possum droppings, mold, mildew, and rubbery toadstools added up to one stinky, yucky (and that is the appropriate word) mess. And to think that my big mouth had put me under that house! I quickly (as you can imagine) added a clean section of flexible duct and cleaned up what mess I could on the way out from under the house.

Did I enjoy it at the time? Strangely enough, by the time I got out I felt blessed that I was physically able to get under the house, that God had given me the ability to fix it, and even that they had let me know about their problem.

And, as if that experience hadn't given me enough joy, the handicapped daughter confided in me that the 'possum's cause of death was buckshot from the laundry room above. Apparently, her mother had fired the gun through the floor to keep out the would-be intruder. I got so tickled I cried all the way home. In my heart I felt truly blessed to be able to worship God by serving my neighbor. Serving (*latreuw*) our neighbors is most definitely a way to present our bodies as a living sacrifice to God (Romans 12:1,2).

While I admit picking some off-the-wall examples for the different aspects of worship, I do want to show how the biblical principle of worship may be different than originally presumed.

Before continuing the study with the following chapter on the word *together*, this may be a good opportunity for you to read the worship-hour account found in Appendix B. As you read the account, think about what goes on during your "worship hour." If you really look around the assembly, you might be surprised to see what is going on while you are "worshiping." I was very surprised.

6

Together Word
Study

*"All the believers were together and had everything in
common."*

(Acts 2:44)

After completing the word study in the previous chapters and reading Appendix B describing an observation
of the worship hour, I hope it is now apparent that our worship should not be relegated to the two or three hours we meet
together at the church building. Meeting together, however,
must still play a key role in the activities of Christians.

With that in mind, let's continue with our word study by
looking at the following passages containing *together* and try
to get a glimpse of what the early Christians did when they
met together. The format is similar to the previous word
study. Parenthetical statements after each scripture place
the word in context, and in some cases, draw out points
that might otherwise go unnoticed.

"For where two or three come together in my name, there am I with them." (Matthew 18:20)

(Note the phrase "together in my name"—don't add "to worship;" it's not there. This could be for anything, even a group of Christians car pooling together, if the reason they are together is because they are Christians.)

"They all joined together constantly in prayer, along with the women and Mary the mother of Jesus, and with his brothers." (Acts 1:14)

(They all prayed together. All includes women—even Mary, the mother of Jesus.)

"When the day of Pentecost came, they were all together in one place." (Acts 2:1)

(Based on previous context, they probably prayed together.)

"Every day they continued to meet together in the temple courts. They broke bread in their homes and ate together with glad and sincere hearts . . . ." (Acts 2:46)

(They met together daily in the temple courts. Then they broke bread and ate together in homes. "[B]roke bread" is the Lord's Supper that was eaten in homes even though they met daily in the temple courts.)

"When they heard this, they raised their voices together in prayer to God." (Acts 4:24)

(They prayed—out loud—together.)

"The apostles performed many miraculous signs and wonders among the people. And all the believers used to meet together in Solomon's Colonnade." (Acts 5:12)

(This doesn't say what the believers were doing, but it sounds like it was a regular occurrence. In one analogy, the relationship between Solomon's Colonnade and the temple would be the same as that of a school parking lot and a school building. The Colonnade would be in the same proximity as the temple courts. So one thing they probably were not doing was eating the Lord's Supper, since they were doing that in their homes.)

"On arriving there, they gathered the church together and reported all that God had done through them and how he had opened the door of faith to the Gentiles." (Acts 14:27)

(They met for the purpose of listening to announcements and missionary reports. Today, congregations often try to minimize these during an assembly.)

"The men were sent off and went down to Antioch, where they gathered the church together and delivered the letter. The people read it and were glad for its encouraging message." (Acts 15:30, 31)

(They gathered to hear someone read a letter from a missionary.)

"A number who had practiced sorcery brought their scrolls together and burned them publicly. When they calculated the value of the scrolls, the total came to fifty thousand drachmas." (Acts 19:19)

(When they met, sinning Christians openly and unashamedly confessed and repented.)

"On the first day of the week we came together to break bread." (Acts 20:7)

(They met to break bread, whatever that means: open the Word of God, eat a meal together, or partake of the Lord's Supper, we can't positively tell from the context. This doesn't say that the first day of the week was the only time they met to break bread or that they did it every first day of the week.)

"Three days later he called together the leaders of the Jews. When they had assembled, Paul said to them: 'My brothers, although I have done nothing against our people or against the customs of our ancestors, I was arrested in Jerusalem and . . . .'" (Acts 28:17)

(They met for an administrative meeting.)

"Pray that I may be rescued from the unbelievers in Judea and that my service in Jerusalem may be acceptable to the saints there, so that by God's will I may come to you with joy and together with you be refreshed." (Romans 15:31, 32)

(They met to be refreshed after a long separation.)

"In the first place, I hear that when you come together as a church, there are divisions among you, and to some extent I believe it. No doubt there have to be differences among you to show which of you have God's approval. When you come together, it is not the Lord's Supper you eat . . . ." (1 Corinthians 11:18–20) (Also in verses 33–34)

(They met to eat the Lord's Supper, supposedly, but Paul said they weren't eating *the Lord's* Supper, because they weren't thinking about the Lord's body—his church. It doesn't say it in this passage, but when they were eating the Lord's supper it was more likely in someone's home than at Solomon's Colonnade. See Acts 2:46 above.)

"So if the whole church comes together and everyone speaks in tongues, and some who do not understand or some unbelievers come in, will they not say that you are out of your mind?" (1 Corinthians 14:23)

(They met to speak in tongues [to edify].)

"What then shall we say, brothers? When you come together, everyone has a hymn, or a word of instruction, a revelation, a tongue or an interpretation. All of these must be done for the strengthening of the church." (1 Corinthians 14:26)

(They met to edify.)

"After that, we who are still alive and are left will be caught up together with them in the clouds to meet the Lord in the air. And so we will be with the Lord forever." (1 Thessalonians 4:17)

(Paul says Christians will be "flying" up to Jesus together.)

"Let us not give up meeting together, as some are in the habit of doing, but let us encourage one another and all the more as you see the Day approaching." (Hebrews 10:25)

(They met to spur one another on, or to challenge each other [Hebrews 10:24]. I have never been gouged by a spur myself, but I assume it probably doesn't feel great. Today, we sometimes take spurring on only in the negative sense.)

After reading the full context of these verses in your Bible, complete the Discussion/Application Questions in Appendix A. Before going on to the next section, write down a few conclusions of your own. May I remind you, again, that this study is intended to be a process by which *you* come to conclusions, rather than a treatise in which *I* make conclusions for you.

PART III:
IMPLICATIONS
OF BIBLICAL
WORSHIP

Why study a topic like worship if only for the aesthetic value? That's what the Areopagus club did on Mars Hill (Acts 17:19). True benefit and fulfillment come from assimilating the information, developing conclusions, and trying to apply what we learn.

One way to describe the possible current worship mindset of some is this. The attendee subconsciously considers presence at the worship hour a hardship (a sacrificial service or activity, *latreuw*). The encompassing worship activity (whether it be listening, praying, giving, etc.) is then also considered the *proskunew* or bowing down (doing what God says to do). This might justify the otherwise redundant term "worship service"—the hour that we serve by bowing down to him because he commands us to do so. The problem with this view, as I now understand worship, is that obeying his commands (serving him) is the *latreuw* form of worship. *Proskunew* worship could never be commanded because it is a condition or outpouring of the heart. It is true that at the name of Jesus every knee shall bow. I don't see it happening at gunpoint, but at a final realization of who he is.

7

Priority and Purpose of Assembly

"Let us not give up meeting together, as some are in the habit
of doing, but let us encourage one another . . ."

(Hebrews 10:25)

If we were to survey congregations across the country we would probably hear several reasons for why people assemble at the church building on Sunday. Some of those reasons may include: because I have to, to make my family happy, because there is nothing else to do, out of habit, to see my friends, to take the Lord's Supper, or to learn more about God. Without a doubt, however, the most common response would be to worship God.

Visitors may or may not be a common sight at your congregation, but even if there aren't visitors to greet and encourage, there are members who are hurting but keep their burdens quiet until some caring soul (like you) talks with them and makes them feel like part of the body. My first reason for assembling, selfish as it may be, would probably be to be encouraged by the singing. Although, depending on the congregation, the singing may be better at a home study group than in the assembly.

Early Church Accounts

Tertullian, an apologist who wrote around 200 A.D., described the first purpose for a Christian assembly was to pray in numbers. Other purposes included to read the "sacred texts," to "arouse hope," to "rebuke and censure" those that have sinned, and to sing (Ferguson 1971, 82). Tertullian mentioned giving only in passing as he explained that the leaders didn't demand it, but said Christians gave only if they wanted on the "*monthly* day" [emphasis added].

Many other apostolic fathers and apologists have also written about Christian assemblies. While these second century writings are not the holy Word of God, they do agree with what the Scriptures say. Let's categorize some of the purposes of assembling together. From what I gathered in my research, a typical assembly would have included: fellowshipping and encouraging other Christians, reading the sacred texts, taking the Lord's supper, confessing sins and verbalizing commitments, being encouraged, making contact with visiting seekers, and praying as one voice to God.

One Vision of a 21st Century Church

Now, if I may indulge you a little further, imagine an assembly where the activities just listed were developed as the primary purpose for assembly, as opposed to "worship God." What spiritual changes might occur if these activities became the purposes of our assemblies? Here's one vision of what Sunday assemblies could look like. I am not suggesting this should be the format for your congregation or even that my dream congregation would be like this. I am only presenting one possible vision of how a congregation could format their assembly based on the apologists' writings.

Fellowship and Encourage Other Christians

After *latreuw* worshiping out in the world and away from the body, we are probably drained spiritually. Just the sight of our brothers and sisters in Christ begins to renew the energy within us. After giving each arriving family member a hug and a kiss, we tell each other about our spiritual war stories, the victories along with the losses. Rather than an auditorium with pews all facing the same direction, the meeting place is more like a restaurant or an airline terminal. We visit for maybe an hour or two—there wasn't a set time, so we couldn't make a statement by being late or early.

Some have brought food to share. Others are talking about physical needs rather than spiritual topics. Even during this fellowship time, Christians seem to want to serve each other in any way they can. Some couples are studying the Bible together privately . . .

Read the Sacred Texts

. . . while a couple of regular teachers discuss specific topics they have prepared. Others are answering specific questions of those not in the focused gatherings. At some point during the fellowship . . .

Take the Lord's Supper

. . . the Lord's Supper is presented on a table. Someone publicly blesses the bread and cup (and possibly anything else that may seem appropriate during the fellowship meal) and conversations change to what Christ has done for humanity and "us" as we begin to eat the bread and drink the cup. Also during this time . . .

Confess Sins and Verbalize Commitments

. . . those who have had "really rough" weeks having been battered by Satan, confess their weaknesses, verbally commit to doing better in the future, and ask others for accountability in the days and weeks to come. Those who are not confessing are hearing confessions. (Those who aren't confessing this week will be doing so in the near future—we are all humans here.) We gain strength from knowing how much our spiritual family cares for us . . .

Be Encouraged

. . . encourages us and we find peace and joy in the assembly. Someone starts singing a favorite song and the crowd begins a song service [*latreuw*] that not only encourages each other, but simultaneously becomes a sweet aroma to God. While we know most everyone in the assembly . . .

Make Contact with Visiting Seekers

. . . some faces are new. They look around with amazement at the contentment and peace of mind that the assembly is exuding. No wonder, the visitors are hearing the best sermon ever preached—love in action. As we continue visiting, a few of the brothers have been systematically surveying the assembly, asking for visitor names and relationships to their hosts . . .

Pray as One Voice to God

. . . as well as any other specific prayer requests. Finally, the entire assembly gathers in close and humbly bows to their Maker in prayer. In one voice and in one accord, we ask for favor and blessings, strength and guidance, healing and cleansing, protection, and perseverance. And, without a doubt, we'll know that we have been to the mountain of the Lord to worship.

Summary

After completing the worship word study it becomes apparent that "worship service" can be a redundant term. If we are going to call Bible things by Bible names, maybe the term *prayer meeting* of fifty years ago or *fellowship meeting* is more appropriate. And if fellowship and encouragement became the primary purpose of the assembly, maybe the entire idea of the church building should be considered. Actually, if fellowship and encouragement became the primary purpose of the assembly, there would probably be more *proskunew* and *latreuw* worship going on as well.

Today, outside influences play a part in molding the physical and organizational structure of the church. The annual budget has items directly attributed to civil and federal law. Even if not required by law, other items such as liability insurance are now sometimes considered "social responsibility." Not stopping there, our own materialistic nature tends to creep into the budget with better environmental controls, more aesthetically pleasing colors, decorations, etc.

My argument is not to simply say that because we have buildings, we have all these additional financial and social distractions. While that may be true, I would rather have us consider whether the building itself, in its current functional status, may be a financial and social distraction to the genuine fellowship and mission of the church. This is better explained in the following chapter.

8

Disadvantages of Buildings as Places of Worship

"Let's build a great city with a tower that reaches to the skies—a monument to our greatness! This will bring us together . . ."
(Genesis 11:4, NLT)

Arguments exist on both sides of the issue of whether physical buildings are appropriate for the Lord's church. As previously stated, the a capella singing group, AVB, has taught much of the brotherhood that "you can't go to church 'cause the church is you." And, in the *mind* of most Christians, this concept is well understood. 1 Corinthians 12 explains that Christ is the head and the church is his body. Further, language throughout the New Testament shows that church refers to people not buildings, or even locations. 1 Corinthians 3 may be comparing individual Christians to building materials. There is also an analogy in 1 Peter 2:5 that refers to the church as a building, but nowhere does it say to build a physical building. For a study on the multi contextual definitions of church see Appendix C.

Some of the points below categorized as disadvantages may, by some, be considered advantages instead. That's okay. The main point of this exercise is not to start burning down church buildings. In the spirit of continuous improvement, we do, however, need to make the most of what we have. So as you read and consider this section, have an open mind and don't think that I am asking you to jump to any hasty conclusions. Critical thinking requires investigating alternatives. The only reason I devote so much attention to buildings is that in such a large number of congregations so much emphasis is currently being placed on buildings.

Disadvantages of Buildings

1. Buildings create formality that undermines biblical worship.
2. Buildings cost money.
3. Buildings encourage materialism (fancy auditorium, fancy clothes, etc.).
4. Buildings are the source of much quarreling on how to use the building.
5. Buildings seem to create observers rather than participants and worshipers.
6. Buildings help tradition become law.
7. Buildings institutionalize.
8. Buildings make "control" easier.
9. Buildings tend to limit the perceived time of "worship" to time spent in the building.
10. Buildings instill the wrong impression of worship.

Of course, we all know that buildings don't do any of these things; people do these things. Please do not read this section as a negative hit on any person or congregation that may be thinking exactly opposite of this. And, before reading the immediately following section discussing these disadvantages, commit to also read the subsequent unit on how to overcome these disadvantages. Most of the examples cited below come from personal experiences. In many of them, I was the one with the wrong understanding. In all of the examples, those involved were of pure motives and had hearts for the Lord. In nearly every case, the situations either have improved or have been completely resolved because of the great congregational leadership and love for the Lord.

Buildings Create Formality that Undermines Biblical Worship

Because of the emphasis placed on "God is not the author of confusion," so much structure is developed that children and outside observers notice the focus on order rather the focus on God that the ceremony is supposed to create. Recall the worship hour observation (Appendix B) and think about how the worship structure tended to create so much attention that those who should have been given attention were being ignored.

Jesus specifically identified as hypocritical the flaunting of special clothing for worship. James also discussed, negatively, the way the rich were given special preference during an assembly. While it is impossible to judge the motives of others, it does seem to be harder to identify with a man in the foyer dressed in jeans and a tee-shirt when one is wearing a business suite and a tie. Yet, I have been told that I was not allowed to "participate in the leading of the worship service" (by carrying communion trays during the Lord's Supper) unless I had a tie on. In another congregation there was a special coat rack storing extra ties so that anyone not appropriately dressed would still be able to "wait at the table" by adding a tie to his attire.

Buildings Cost Money

The purpose of the collection often stated during the time of giving is to help the needy and evangelize the world. Yet if one were to break down the typical annual congregational budget it would probably reveal that most of the congregational funds were being divided between facilities and staff salaries. Some secular nonprofit organizations are sometimes chided because of the low percent of funds that make it to the needy or disadvantaged, but most congregations actually have a smaller percentage of their budget going to helping the needy and evangelizing the lost.

Some buildings cost all this money and are only used for four or five hours per week—three on Sunday, one on Wednesday evening, and possibly a ladies' Bible class. While this may now be the exception rather than the rule, even the most activity-filled buildings have much empty time. Then there are other costs like long-term building maintenance, housekeeping or janitorial services, parking lot repaving and sealing, mortgage interest, insurance—it's not a church building; it's a business.

Buildings Encourage Materialism

Keeping up with the Jones is easy compared to having to match the majesty of a cathedral or even staying abreast of the facility improvements of the community church down the street. From padded pews to plush pulpits, the building is a giant vacuum of congregational funds. Whether originating from Old Testament temple instructions, the Catholic-Protestant tradition, or just human nature in general, churches seem to want to make the building the glory of the congregation, and emphasize most a formal or elegant auditorium.

Banks and insurance companies often have buildings that are said by their architects to embody and present the image of the company. Being a quantitative kind of guy, I generally look at those same buildings and get the resentful feeling that, if they had enough money for a building like that they could have given me a lower interest rate on my loan or reduced my premiums. Church buildings are sometimes no different. Rather than trying to surround ourselves with humility, we attempt to lavish ourselves with luxury—in the name of giving to God. That's what diner's clubs and country clubs are for, not churches. Many commentaries explain it differently, but, to me, James chapters four and five seem to address Christians specifically on this matter.

It is possible that congregations are only functioning the same as the majority of their members—spending the money for self rather than for others. Yes, arguments could be made for making an impression on outsiders, but what impression is it? That we put priority on physical possessions? Attend here because we spend money on us?

And, of course, because we spend so much money on the building, we want to protect it (Luke 12:34, "For where your treasure is, there your heart will be also."). So rather than trusting God to protect it, we buy insurance policies that restrict our freedom by requiring us to limit access to the building. Soon we get the idea to lock the playground so only certain children can play on it. We wouldn't want the neighborhood children playing on the playground (they might be injured), and we surely wouldn't want to take a chance on a homeless person keeping warm or dry in the lobby at night. In addition to physical security, buildings often become an emotional security. And if you disagree on how much insurance we should have on a building and whether outsiders should tell us how to use the building, I'm not surprised. Read the next heading.

Buildings Are the Source of Much Quarreling on How to Use the Building

Whether in the northern United States or in the southern so-called "Bible belt" there are congregations at odds over the sinfulness, or at least the inappropriateness, of using the building or church property for potluck fellowships, scout troop meetings, Christian academies, and basketball hoops in parking lots—God forbid even considering something such as a gymnasium on the church grounds. Rather than stir the pot (any more) on these topics it should be enough to simply mention them as a reminder of how building usage is the source of much quarreling.

Another example of quarreling over buildings is as simple as what the main assembly location should be called. It was on a Wednesday evening at least fifteen minutes before the short devotional was to begin before being dismissed to Bible classes. I was loitering in the church office (notice even this nomenclature is misleading relative to biblical terminology) when a young, newly-married woman came to me literally bawling. After finally calming her down enough that she could talk, she asked if "we" had to call the [assembly room] the auditorium or could we also call it the sanctuary? It actually happened that she was asking an older lady in the church about such and such in the "sanctuary," and, rather than answering the young lady's question, the older lady sharply rebuked her in the use of the word sanctuary spouting, "Baptists call it a sanctuary, but it is an auditorium and you had better call it an auditorium." Hopefully, this is not how all older women teach the younger women.

Buildings Seem to Create Observers Rather than Participants and Worshipers

Choirs during the "worship service" are rejected by some Christian religious movements because it is thought that the congregation is the choir and that all members are participants. At least that is what is being preached. What is being practiced in many congregations, however, is a de facto choir where those in the choir are the ones singing (maybe as few as half of the congregation). The remaining observers are talking, chewing gum, daydreaming, trying to make children behave, or otherwise not being part of the choir.

The stereotypical nudge in the husband's ribs may also indicate something less than participation. I suppose even observers may get more from the lesson than sleepers. To avoid sleepiness or maybe even boredom, some take walks to the restroom or lobby, as if it were a chore to sit through the service. Each seemingly inconsequential activity tells something about how we view the worship hour. Even the rebuking the young lady received for calling the auditorium a sanctuary reveals much about the way people really feel about the building—that it is a place to come to listen, observe, and be entertained (auditorium) rather than to participate in fellowship in holy protection (sanctuary) as a body of believers.

Buildings Help Tradition Become Law

Preachers behind pulpits, audiences, foyers—even the mystical area behind the podium and the baptismal dressing rooms may derive much of their meaning from the design of the building. Several seemingly innocuous laws I remember deal with use of the building. "Thou shalt not run in the auditorium as it is the place of worship." "Thou shalt no go up near the podium as that is where the preacher stands." You know them as well. Most may never have been written down. Some may never have been worded as a law. But they nonetheless helped form our inaccurate view of the significance of the building as a place of worship.

Buildings petrify traditions into laws of stone, when pews are thought to be scripturally required, when the desired songbooks are not purchased because they would not fit properly into the pew racks, and when those leading the morning prayer are required to go to the front of the building because that is where the microphone is wired in. Could any of these laws be changed with little effort? Of course they could. They won't be changed, however, because of the authority that the building maintains, simply because it's a building and we are human. (This situation truly calls for us to "think outside of the building.")

In the past I had trouble seeing how this could possibly be true. It is similar to poor, homeless, jobless persons wondering in the downtown district of a large city. Why do they continue to beg for money? Why don't they just get a job at a fast food joint or get a bus ticket out of the city where the cost of living isn't so high and they can find a better job?

More recently, I have come to realize that although environment doesn't have to dictate actions, it almost always affects mindset. And I truly believe it may not be within poor beggars' abilities to conceive, or believe if told, that they could easily transport themselves to better situations. The same may be true with buildings. It may not be possible to conceive that the building might look better if the ceiling were painted white rather than brown because for the last thirty years it has been painted brown. It has become law, unquestionable law, to be defended at all costs.

Buildings Institutionalize

Because of the physical size of some congregations, especially in the south, whatever they do will be accepted by surrounding congregations. Of course, there are also those congregations who will say, "Because that 'liberal' church did it doesn't mean we should do it also." The appropriate time of worship is Sunday morning 9:00 or 10:00 A.M., Sunday night at 6:00 P.M., and Wednesday night at 7:00 P.M. Nearly any congregation in the United States holds services during these (institutionally) approved times. On one hand, there is a proclamation that "we" are nondenominational, and that each congregation is autonomous. (Find either of those two big words in the Bible.) Yet on the other hand, there are conventions, lectureships, universities, and conferences that would rival any acknowledged denominational institution or synod.

A more local example of the way churches institutionalize would be the use of financial vouchers that must be requested with a signature, approved by the deacon in charge of that ministry with a signature, and be approved by the deacon of finance (yes, with another signature), before the elder "initials off" and the funds can be dispersed. And according to sociologist and author, Neil Postman (Postman 1992), institutions are nothing more than a way to control people and their ideas. More specifically, this form of institution is called a bureaucratic institution. The idea of the church as a bureaucratic institution will be explored further in the next section.

Many church buildings have an "elders' room." One in particular that I am thinking of used to be a nursery. It still has the Noah's Ark mural painted on the wall. It now has—in addition to the nursery theme mural—two conference tables and more than a half dozen black leather executive swivel chairs. The new makeshift nursery was a bit crowded at first, but it wasn't long before the nursery

attendance decreased to fit the size of the new room. The
subconscious corporate mentality of church leadership may
be perpetuated by the existence of buildings.

Buildings Make "Control" Easier

In a different situation, a conflict once arose about the
scripturalness of having small groups (called home Bible
studies to relieve some of the tension). During a special
men's meeting called to discuss the problem, two reasons
against having small groups on Sunday evening were: 1)
Small groups will introduce false doctrine into the church;
and 2) small groups scatter the congregation preventing
the eldership from being able to adequately shepherd the
flock. The first opposing argument was quickly settled by
asking how small groups on Tuesday night (which had been
hypothetically approved) would not introduce false doctrine, but having the groups meet on Sunday night would
allow false doctrine to infiltrate. The second argument had
more tradition behind it and took more convincing, but
clear scriptural examples of house churches showed that
first century elders somehow managed to shepherd the
flock even when scattered throughout house churches in a
city the size of Ephesus. As cited in the *Holman Dictionary*,
Ephesus is estimated to have had a population of around
250,000 during the New Testament period.

Refer to Appendix C for additional study on churches
and a possible interpretation of how elders could govern
cities, not just single congregations. Although never
stated specifically, the underlying issue of the argument
against the home Bible studies was really one of control.
Admittedly, it is easier to manage a group of people when

they are under one roof. Many do not understand the difference between shepherding, which involves leading and protecting, and managing, which involves scheduling and controlling.

Buildings Can Limit the Perceived Time of "Worship" to Time Spent in the Building

Continuing to use insights gained from the home Bible study scenario, it was apparent that those opposing them did not believe that worship would be taking place unless it was being done in the building. Preachers, song leaders, and other announcers also perpetuate this idea as they encourage or exhort the congregation to "come back for worship tonight" and to "make plans to return on Wednesday for services." Even those preachers who know, intellectually at least, that worship can take place outside of the building continue to emphasize coming back to the building to worship.

Buildings Instill the Wrong Impression of Worship

As Jesus discussed the issue of buildings with the Samaritan woman at the well in John 4, he made it clear there was not a place of worship, but that true worshipers would worship in spirit (that is, non-physically) and in truth (truthfully or genuinely). By requiring a building for a place of worship, are we not, in a sense, reverting back to some of the very same burdens that Christ has freed us from? In Galatians 4:9, Paul explained, "But now that you know

God—or rather are known by God—how is it that you are turning back to those weak and miserable principles? Do you wish to be enslaved by them all over again?" By making the place of worship our heart rather than a building, God frees us. By making the building a place of worship we are enslaving ourselves and hampering the true worship Jesus refers to in John 4.

Even in the Old Testament, the prescribed place of worship was a tent, not an ornate temple. And when David felt bad living in a "cedar palace" and wanted to build a permanent structure for God, God's reply was, "I have not dwelt in a house from the day I brought Israel up out of Egypt to this day. I have moved from one tent site to another, from one dwelling place to another. Wherever I have moved with all the Israelites, did I ever say to any of their leaders whom I commanded to shepherd my people, 'Why have you not built me a house of cedar?'" (1 Chronicles 17:5–6). It seems as though God was only graciously accepting man's idea of a permanent dwelling place on earth even though he knew it couldn't begin to contain him. King Solomon's wisdom was apparent when he later dedicated the temple and said, "But will God really dwell on earth with men? The heavens, even the highest heavens, cannot contain you. How much less this temple I have built!" (2 Chronicles 6:18). When the nation wanted a king, God warned of the dangers of having a king and considered the nation to be rejecting him as their leader (1 Samuel 8:6,7). But he still allowed it. Similarly, when man wanted to build a building for God to dwell in, it seems as if God was saying, "That is not necessary since I am spirit—not flesh. But since you are like a child and don't understand, I will let you build me a building." Again,

Jesus explained this several centuries later in John 4:21–24. He essentially said there is no longer a place for worship because worship is non-physical.

Having a building as a place of worship instills the concept that worship is physical when Jesus says it is non-physical. At least until the mindset of the people changes, it appears that the building could be used as a crutch and may be a hindrance to biblical worship.

Silence of the Scriptures Regarding Church Buildings

Why is it that some Christians take silence of the scripture regarding musical instruments in worship as authoritative, yet sometimes spend over half the congregational budget on buildings which are never mentioned other than the meeting in Herod's temple (Acts 5:12), an Old Testament vestige? It doesn't even say in this example that they were worshiping in Solomon's Colonnade, which was as much courtyard as it was building. The Greek word *aineo* usually translated as *praise* is used in Luke 24:53 to convey the idea that the disciples hung around the temple telling each other stories about the good things that God had done, but even this was before the establishment of the church as recorded in Acts 2. And even if they were worshiping there; it wasn't the Christians' property, but more of a public commons area. Church buildings today, however, are not only considered *expedient*, but a necessity.

Both the issue of instrumental music and places of worship have similar Old Testament heritages. That is, they both were not only allowed, but prescribed in the Old Testament

(Exodus 25:9, Nehemiah 12:36). Yet, in the New Testament they are conspicuously absent. In the case of instrumental music, the absence is taken by most congregations affiliated with the churches of Christ movement (and others, such as the Greek Orthodox Church) as a forbiddance. In the case of buildings, the absence is explained away by such logic as, "They were a new organization and had not gotten around to building them," or "They were a very poor group of people and couldn't afford buildings."

Opposite arguments would be just as logical. "Musical instruments would have been fine, but they didn't have them because they were always having to meet under-ground and couldn't take a chance of being caught." And, "There was plenty of money for buildings. Many Christians held prominent positions in the cities (Acts 17:4,12) and, as people had need, property was sold and given to the church (Acts 4:36–37), it's just that buildings were not desired by God. The issue is not mentioned in the New Testament because it was so obvious to the Christians that they were not to be built."

This immediate discussion is not to rule on the possible issue of whether instrumental music should be a part of Christian assemblies, but it does make me think again about the appropriateness of buildings as places of worship. I am not insisting that the ultimate answer for some congregations may actually be to sell their building and begin meeting in homes or public facilities. I do know of fellowships where this has been done successfully. There are also significant examples where groups turn into cults, or near cults, and happen not to have buildings.

Change for the sake of change is not good. And there should be much prayer and fasting before a decision like that is made. On the other hand, please don't just dismiss this discussion of church buildings as loony, without thinking about where we got the idea for them in the first place. The following chapter and Appendix D should help you with this.

9

Bureaucracy of the Modern Church Organization

"They tie up heavy loads and put them on men's shoulders, but they themselves are not willing to lift a finger to move them. Everything they do is done for men to see: They make their phylacteries wide and the tassels on their garments long; they love the place of honor at banquets and the most important seats in the synagogues; they love to be greeted in the marketplaces and to have men call them 'Rabbi.'... Woe to you, teachers of the law and Pharisees, you hypocrites! You give a tenth of your spices mint, dill and cummin. But you have neglected the more important matters of the law—justice, mercy and faithfulness. You should have practiced the latter, without neglecting the former. You blind guides! You strain out a gnat but swallow a camel."

(Matthew 23:4–7, 23:23, 24)

Assembling in Church Buildings

Historic records show that during the second and third centuries some of the house churches possibly met in homes with a remodeled room to better accommodate the assembly. But buildings constructed specifically for church assemblies were not constructed until the fourth century (Ferguson 1971, 77). This was about the same time that infant baptism became more widespread. Mattox (Mattox 1961, 126) explained that at this time Constantine not only ordered the persecutions to stop, but authorized state money to build buildings and encouraged the construction of elaborate buildings.

While it could be argued that buildings were not being built before this time because of the easy targets they would make for persecuting Christians, that reasoning would not be consistent with the spirit of the early Christian assemblies mentioned by Ferguson (Ferguson 1971, 77). He indicated the Christians may have thought it was more of a threat not to meet, because of the dangers of spiritual pride or doctrinal divisions, than to meet and face possible persecution. Their philosophy was correctly patterned after the teaching of Jesus, who warned not to fear him who could kill the body, but fear him who could kill both body and soul (Matthew 10:28).

Admittedly, there is no infallible method to determine precisely when church buildings emerged, or for that matter, no definite criteria for knowing when a house church is actually a church house. The point is that church buildings did not become what we know them to be until the government started subsidizing them. From that event on, if not even before, the church has been battling institutionalism and bureaucracy. See Appendix D, Etiology of Current Building/Worship Practice for better closure on this topic. Here, the discussion is bureaucracy in the current church organization; so let's continue.

Bureaucracy As an Organizational Structure

One disadvantage of church buildings was listed as Buildings Institutionalize. Along with the concept of institutions, also comes the concept of the bureaucracy. Developed in France as a method that actually improved governmental administration, it is now generally considered inefficient and used specifically when the intent is to slow progress, thereby preventing unwanted change.

Weber (Weber 1947, cited in Hall 1999) described the ideal bureaucracy as having several elements: a hierarchy of authority, limited authority, division of labor, technically competent participants, procedures for work, rules for incumbents, and differential rewards. Of course, this is the ideal bureaucratic organization. If one element is lacking, the remaining elements will be affected. For example, when the participants (workers) are not competent, division of labor must be reconsidered, rules and procedures have to be changed, etc.

Governmental organizations, like church organizations, are nonprofit, but church organizations are also volunteer organizations. This brings additional obstacles into a bureaucracy. Not only are the members volunteers and stand a chance of being incompetent, but the leaders are sometimes in the same category as well. Examples of bureaucratic inefficiencies are presented below. Often, the reduced efficiency is countered by getting more help, which may again, be incompetent or at least not well suited for the job. The expanding spiral is more damaging than one might expect.

Bureaucracies tend to grow beyond their originally intended bounds. The founding fathers of the United States had much to say about this. In fact, the right to bear arms was intended to protect the citizenry from the government, not from robbers or foreign enemies. I will only cite here the biblical warning given by God about civil bureaucratic governments, (1 Samuel 8), so we can get back to how a different way of thinking about worship may, in practice, change the way the church organization functions.

Manifestations of Bureaucracy in the Church Organization

Many congregations adopt an ad hoc bureaucracy as their organizational structure. The division of labor and procedures for work elements of a bureaucracy imply committees and pigeonholing of problems and their solutions. And, of course, problems and solutions may not be in the same pigeonhole. Without constant effective communication, bureaucracies cannot survive. For this study on worship I must completely avoid any discussion on the invisible hierarchy above the local congregation level, but you can probably imagine where it would lead us.

Following are a few typical examples of how the bureaucratic system, and the general imposition of worldly society can detract from the purposes of the church. Your congregation might not presently deal with any of these issues. If that is the case, let me just say you are blessed. Let me also say in advance that none of these activities are unbiblical, or even are non-biblical. On the contrary, they are, in principle, all well-founded in Scripture. They only detract from the church's mission when they are handled improperly.

Elder Leadership Styles

With much of my formal research being devoted to the difference between leading and managing and their respective values, I would really like to expound on this point, but I will refrain. Let me simply state here that the most effective ways of shepherding the Lord's church may not even be similar to methods used to lead most organizations today. Many congregations have not seen how a shepherd is supposed to lead and consider corporate America to be the example of what leadership is. In fact, when so-called leading takes place in some congregations, it is from those experienced in managing a secular business. It may be the only way the elders know exists. It may even be what the congregation expects—somewhat of a board of directors. This is not, however, what the Bible portrays as leadership, nor is it consistent with the example of leadership Christ gave.

That is not to say that since corporate CEOs plan and implement strategy elders should not. Shepherds are spiritual leaders and are involved in, and concerned about, the spiritual well being of their members. Planning and strategy are good, and probably necessary, but when strategic emphasis is on buildings and operations rather than spiritual lives, we are confused.

Role of Deacons

Having served in the military I have noticed that many elderships (bodies of elders) either view themselves or are viewed by the congregation as the commissioned officers of the church. If that is the case, then the deacons act as the non-commissioned officers of the church organization. A military commissioned officer's role is to lead or manage, depending on rank; a non-commission officer's role is to either manage or supervise, depending on rank. (If you have a military background, I apologize for the slight oversimplification.) In this scenario, the elders then delegate to the deacons the responsibility of managing or supervising programs.

The apostles chose men for the program of feeding widows during the initial phase of the church (Acts 6:1–6). The qualifications for the men to be chosen were only to have a good reputation and to be full of the Holy Spirit and wisdom—definitely not the same qualifications for deacons as listed in Paul's letters to Timothy and Titus. The Greek words *diakonew* (G1247) and *diakonia* (G1248) could mean either to serve or to minister and were used both ways—once in referring to the act of helping the widows (a "physical" program), and once for the work of the apostles in evangelizing (a "spiritual" program).

My perception of Paul's model in 1 Timothy 3 is that deacons are general servants of the church. It could also imply that the deacons are to be mentored by the elders so that the future generations of the church can know and practice spiritual leadership. We don't often see elders "mentoring" deacons, usually only "delegation."

Care Groups

In some congregations the physical duty of taking meals to the hungry has not even been given to the deacons, but to care groups or zone groups. Think about the concept of collecting funds from individual church members so that a few individuals are obliged to fix or buy a meal and take it to someone whom they may have never met, in the name of the church. (For some it seems wrong to take funds from the church treasury for this internal ministry, so members take a separate voluntary collection.) Is this in any way reminiscent of any federal programs we could think of?

Somehow, it seems that a bureaucratic secular society has influenced the "business of the church." Here, the word *latreuw* comes to mind, and it represents a direct conflict with, "Sorry, I gave at the care group meeting." A smaller, more personal organizational structure would empower those who know a sick person to visit them and take them meals. If we have been doing our latreuw properly there won't be members that have no one to visit them and need a welfare-type organization to assist them. We are sometimes influenced so much by society that we can't recognize when it encroaches on true religion.

My understanding of James 1:27 includes more than food and a cursory visit, but "looking after" their emo-tional—and house maintenance—needs as well. The bu-reaucratic response to this is to start more programs for widows' home maintenance, lawn moving, leaf raking, and "appreciation dinners." An alternative response would be to get to know a widow and "look after her in her distress," whatever that may entail. Although not popular in today's global society, the best solution to the problem of organiza-tional management is to have a small, simple organization in the first place. Similarly, church bureaucracies with large programs may be less effective and less efficient in the long run than urging congregation members to be Christians and mentor them as Jesus and Paul did.

Congregational Giving

The typical current protocol of giving instills a "gave at the office" mentality. With biblical worship there would be opportunities to give every day to those in need as well as contributing to the church fund. As it is, the contribution is possibly just another family or personal budget item, just like the FICA (social security tax) that is deducted from each paycheck, and there is no money left for service type worship throughout the week.

Admittedly, current tax laws tend to penalize personally giving to those in need compared donating to charitable 501c3 organizations such as churches. But primarily, it is a mindset that has evolved because: 1) the building is considered the place of worship; and 2) church organization has evolved into a bureaucracy. Biblically speaking we are to do ". . . something useful with [our] own hands, that [we] may have something to share with those in need" (Ephesians 4:48). The implication seems to be that we are to help those in need daily, *as we see their need.* This would not only improve the efficiency of the ministry from maybe 50 percent to 100 percent, but would also allow us to share Christ with those in need—not just food or clothing.

Bible Classes

From my experiences, I have noted that generally only half or two-thirds of those attending a Sunday morning assembly will also come to the associated Bible class. Teachers and leaders sometimes blame those not attending of being disinterested or too immature to understand the need or benefit of Bible class attendance. Maybe we would be more productive by taking a different point of view—that something is inherently wrong with some Bible class systems.

The secular school system is great at taking away our children so they have a better chance at succeeding in this world, without a thought of succeeding in the next. Yet, as school discipline and other issue-oriented topics, such as school prayer, have eroded the effectiveness of the public school system (Howard 1990), we as parents generally feel there is nothing we can do. There is plenty we can do, from the legislative level down to taking the children out of the system to be private or homeschooled.

In the Bible class system, on the other hand, we generally feel that nothing bad can happen to our children. Bible class is only for one hour, they seem to enjoy it, and they are learning at least something about the Bible, so we tend not to concern ourselves with it. But, by not focusing on continuous improvement of the Bible class system, it sometimes becomes just another activity that children participate in, along with piano, soccer, and all the other secular activities.

As the children's classes may for some be a babysitting service, the adult classes may be either a time of relaxation and escape from the business of the week, or the fulfillment of a worship requirement. These rationales being stated, the most common complaint I hear regarding Bible classes is that they aren't "on the Bible." They are often either politically correct social issue discussions, "gab times" as one lady described it to me; or shallow biblical discussions with most of the class time resulting in opinionated stories from the lecturer that keep the communication away from the biblical exhortations and encouragement.

Another trend today is toward Bible classes where the first half of the class is devoted to visiting and telling stories of what happened during the past week followed by a discussion and listing of prayer requests. The five-minute prayer may then terminate with the class bell ringing. Please don't think I am trying to dissuade prayer and visiting. We have already discussed prayer and fellowship as two of the primary purposes for assembling. I do think that because we have so little contact with other Christians throughout the week that the more socially-inclined brothers and sisters feel a stronger hunger for visiting with each other than for the Word of God.

Praise be to God that we are not all the foot, the hand, the eye, the ear, or even the "big toe." My point is that we as teachers or facilitators and students or participants should always be conscience of what we think God wants us to be doing and be continually working toward accomplishing his will.

According to Mac Lynn's research (Lynn 1997), more than 1,100 congregations of the churches of Christ do not have individualized Bible classes. Over 500 of them have no Bible classes. While I have neither recently attended such a congregational assembly nor interviewed the membership, some possible reasons for not having Bible classes may be exactly the bureaucratic, institutional, or societal influence of the basic concept Sunday school is based on. Other reasons might include issues of unity, harmony, leadership control, or lack thereof.

Paradigm Shift

As emphasis is removed from the worship hour, emphasis will also be removed from the building as the center of the church organization. The organization will more likely form a distributed network, where smaller groups of Christians will practice Christianity more effectively and efficiently within their local communities. As this trend develops, more of the world will see firsthand what "abundant life" is, and will want it for themselves. Even the "one vision for a 21st century church," described in a previous chapter, is, in reality, an evolutionary step toward what might actually develop if the concept of biblical worship were to be adopted.

An analogy that might help in understanding this would be the way written communication changes depending on whether it is in paper format or web page format. In the science of printed documents, an advanced system has developed for making communication more effective using that media. Some of these techniques might include the use of certain fonts and sizes, paragraph length, margin space, line spacing, etc. Simply copying the written data and accompanying style to electronic media is one possible implementation method, but after seeing the flexibility and emphasis that is available in web page style, the paper style seems rigid and lacking communicative effectiveness when viewed on a computer display. Text font, color, style, and size barely touch the surface of possibilities of web pages.

In addition to words that blink, flash, change color, or even morph into different words or to icons, the real strength of the new paradigm in writing is the ability to point to, or link to, other areas of the text. For example, if a word is not understood by the reader, the possibility exists for him/her to click on the word and immediately read its definition. Links are also sometimes used to give author information for a cited reference, to expound on a topic, or link to an electronic book that is currently stored on the other side of the world. It is even possible to click on a word and get its associated picture or sound.

The previous vision of a 21st century church is like taking the paper document with its paper document style and putting it in electronic format. With the biblical worship paradigm, we are not restricted to the building as if it were an electronic document using a paper format. But before I give my final vision of the church, we need to investigate some practical approaches to start heading us in the direction of effective change.

PART IV:
IMPLEMENTING
BIBLICAL
WORSHIP

Just for sake of argument, let's suppose that Gulf War II had not turned out to be so decisive and that terrorist activities were common events in the United States. (No reference is being made to the socio-political outcome, only the military outcome.) Assume further that church buildings became primary targets of opportunity. For some congregations, even in the United States, this is not hypothetical. I recall the Black congregations whose buildings were being burnt, and also the church building in or near San Francisco, California, that was being attacked by homosexual rights activists while the members were inside and the police doing nothing to stop it. Is your congregation spiritually, emotionally, and organizationally prepared to survive such events?

In a different scenario, the government could make it unlawful or, at least highly politically incorrect, to meet together at a church building. You can say it won't happen, but that doesn't remove the possibility. Communist block countries weren't always governed by atheist leaders, but for several decades, when they were, Christians had a hard time meeting in church buildings. How would your congregation adapt if forced to go underground?

Adverse scenarios such as the ones just introduced may or may not happen in our lifetime, but, even if they never occur, we could be more effective as congregations if we weren't so tied to our buildings. Once we learn how to worship without having to use the building as a crutch, we might just see the church thriving again. As long as place and procedure are paramount, people will always be left behind. However, once our priorities are in order, there are still several ways to make the building useful.

10

Overcoming Disadvantages of Buildings

"And whatever you do, whether in word or deed, do it all in the name of the Lord Jesus, giving thanks to God the Father through him."

(Colossians 3:17)

New Covenant Sanctuary

Now the first covenant had regulations for worship and also an earthly sanctuary (Hebrews 9:1). We can read about the regulations for worship in the Old Testament books of Law. We also can see what God prescribed as his sanctuary, although what he prescribed was much less elaborate than what the nation of Israel ultimately built. In fact, by Jesus' day, Herod's temple grounds were roughly the size of twenty-five football fields and took more than a half-century to build!

Around A.D. 70 the Roman Empire destroyed the temple as Christ predicted. And before that, Christ removed the wall of partition into the inner sanctuary allowing us full access to it—the real sanctuary, not the earthly shadow (Hebrews 10). As if access to the true sanctuary of God weren't enough, he has also made us, as individuals, sanctuaries by allowing the Spirit to live in us (Romans 8:11, and others).

Not only did God tell us that the new sanctuary was us; he also told us that the place for worship was us. Today, our "regulations for worship" are found in John 4:23 and Romans 12:1, 2. Jesus said true worshipers would worship in spirit (that is, non-physically) and in truth (truthfully or genuinely). Let's look again at John 4:20f. The woman at the well was specifically asking about the proper location of worship. Although Jesus only said that it was in neither place she asked about, it seems clear after reading the rest of the context that he was saying there will be *no* physical place of worship because each person will be worshiping at the spiritual sanctuary located within each Christian. This concept may seem like a lot to grasp due to our preoccupation with buildings, but should become clearer as we continue to develop the old/new covenant analogy. (I realize am going against my "no redundancy" philosophy with my repeated use of John 4, but as you can see, it is critical to the study. Also, because the passage is sometimes also used to support the requirement of "correct" worship procedures rather than the concept Jesus was apparently explaining, I want to explain it several times.)

Our Role as Priests

The writer of Hebrews compares the newly obsolete priestly order of Aaron to that of Melchizedek, but primarily focuses on the role Jesus plays in the latter order. That was fine for the recipients of the initial document as it proved the supremacy of Christ (and the new covenant) over the old covenant. So, what is our role as priests?

Let's continue our worship analogy with respect to priestly duties by comparing high priest, priest, area of service, and articles of sacrifice as points of interest. Under the Law, the high priest was Aaron or one of his direct descendants. Other priests were those selected from the tribe of Levi. Their area of service was the Israelite nation, and they worked throughout that area (e.g., collecting tithes, Nehemiah 10:37,38), not just at the temple. The general articles of sacrifice were items brought to the temple by the nation of Israel.

Some specific articles of sacrifice were burned by the priests in the temple. Several times in the Old Testament, God noticed the sweet-smelling smoke from the sacrifices as it rose up to heaven and called it a pleasing aroma to him. Leviticus and Numbers mention this nearly three dozen times. Christ was the burnt offering for sin. His crucifixion was that sacrifice. But, not all of the sacrifices were burnt offerings. For example, drink offerings were poured out rather than burned.

Today we have a high priest, Christ (Hebrews 6:20). We are the priests and offer spiritual sacrifices (1 Peter 2:5). And, as in the Old Testament, we can use the analogy of smoke from our sacrifices rising up to God and being pleasing to him. In one sense, we are the smoke or aroma that rises from the offering (2 Corinthians 2:15). To those who accept it, we smell like perfume; to the others, we smell like death.

There is another sense in which we are like the Old Testament sacrifices. We are drink offerings and are being poured out like wine as we serve and suffer for others. Paul used this analogy a couple of times to explain how his work was worship to the Lord (Philippians 2:17; 2 Timothy 4:6).

There is another sense in which we are not the offering ourselves, but are the priests who are making the offering. In this case, the article of sacrifice is not Jesus or us, but food, clothing, money, etc. This is still worship to the Lord.

The context of Philippians 4 illustrates how Old Testament worship correlates to New Testament worship. Notice the key worship terminology, "the gifts you sent . . . are a fragrant offering, an acceptable sacrifice, pleasing to God" (v. 18). As the Philippians sent help to Paul in the way of material possessions, they were, in the true sense of the word, worshiping God—in this case, *latreuw*, or service-type worship. We can offer other types of sacrifices that would fall into the *proskunew* bowing down or praising worship.

The duties of the priests centered around making sacrifices. It was their service or latreuw. Think about the Catholic priests today when they perform the mass. It is called the liturgy. As priests, our duties also center around making sacrifices. The writer in Hebrews 13:15,16 tells us to worship both ways and uses language that calls it worship: "Through Jesus, therefore, let us continually offer to God a sacrifice of praise the fruit of lips that confess his name. And do not forget to do good and to share with others, for with such sacrifices God is pleased."

Again, Paul is using the worship analogy when he tells us to "to offer [our] bodies as living sacrifices, holy and pleasing to God this is [our] spiritual act of worship" (Romans 12:1). After seeing so many references to our daily lives being worship to God, and how the worship involves sacrificing, it really makes me wonder how we could have been thinking all this time that we only worship in the building—even if that is the way we have done it for the last 1,700 years.

The requirement to come to a specific location to offer sacrifices is definitely present in the Old Testament, as part of the old Law. But is also explained as a shadow and not the reality that is found in Christ. "The law is only a shadow of the good things that are coming not the realities themselves" (Hebrews 10:1). Colossians 2:17 explains that the reality is found in Christ, not in the assemblies and festivals that were part of the Jewish system of religion.

Well, it doesn't look good for me. I was supposed to be discussing advantages of buildings when it sounds like all I have done is continue discussing how we don't need them. But, in reality, once we understand our role as priests, and who it is we are supposed to be serving, that is, our area of service, the advantages of buildings should become apparent: They're just buildings like any other buildings, do whatever you want in them!

To those who come to the building thinking it is a holy location of God, serve them and let them know that God is present there (because he can be present anywhere). To the non-Christians who would not otherwise associate with Christians, have Boy Scout meetings, sponsor Al-Anon meetings, start a daycare center, and do whatever else you can think of that will allow you to show Christ to the world, which is your area of service. Since the human high priest was eliminated, everything has moved up a notch toward closer access to God. The whole nation of God is now the priesthood and the world is now the area of service.

General Suggestions (Dos and Don'ts)

I hesitate to mention specifics here because of the chance they will be taken as limiting factors in what congregations can do. Hopefully, you will use this list only as a springboard to find ways of serving God by helping others and praising him.

Don't be afraid to do things in the building that are not wrong. Laughing, being joyful, and having fun are not wrong. God likes it when we do these things.

Don't be afraid to miss worship hour to help or encourage someone who needs it.

Don't allow the disadvantages to takeover.

Do spend more time at the building doing things other than traditional worship.

Do be courageous and use the building for doing good, whatever that might be.

Do use the building as a tool for biblical worship.

Do use the building any way possible to evangelize.

Do make necessary changes to the physical structure of the building so it can be effective for biblical worship.

It is not my intent to ban buildings or to stop meeting together as Christians. I do want us to begin considering other times of the week as worship, and focus more on the personal (private) aspect of worship, since, in fact, that is what worship is. My guess is that when this occurs, "public worship," in whatever form it may take, will actually be more rewarding and inspirational. And this is the goal many have been trying to accomplish all along.

In the introductory chapter, I mentioned that several books had recently been written on worship, but dealt primarily creating more inspiring "worship services." I am guessing the authors' philosophies have been that if we create an inspiring worship service, those who attend will be more spiritual throughout the week. My view appears to be just the opposite (actually, the converse): that if we can convince Christians that worship is what we do for others because of God and how we think about God, then our fellowship time together *will* be inspiring no matter what we do during those times together.

Keeping the Spirit Alive

"Do not stifle the Holy Spirit."

(1 Thessalonians 5:19, NLT)

Biblical Worship as a Way of Life

When we understand the biblical pattern for worshiping, we will make better use of our time. Paul explains in 2 Corinthians 5 that since he understands who God is, he is all the more motivated to tell others about him. In fact, he doesn't look at anyone from a worldly perspective any longer, but sees everyone as a soul to be won for Christ. Paul seems to have incorporated worship into every aspect of his life. Part of his motivation was fear (*phobew*, 2 Corinthians 5:11). He also admitted to Felix, the governor, that he was a worshiper (*latreuw*) of God (Acts 24:14). His daily service to the saints was *latreuw* (Romans 12:1,2).

It was interesting to me to find that of the seventy-two times *proskunew* is used in the New Testament, Paul only uses it once, and in that case, he is referring to an outsider who begins to worship when he sees Christians acting properly (Paul doesn't use any word for worship). The word appears only four times in Acts; once in reference to a false God, once to Peter (where he had to correct Cornelius), and twice where individuals had gone to Jerusalem to worship. It is used twice in Hebrews: where angels are told to worship (Hebrews 1:6); and when Jacob worshiped as he leaned on his staff (Hebrews 11:21). Besides these seven times, all other 65 instances of the word are found in the Gospels and Revelation. It seems that this type of worship is more prevalent when in the physical presence of God. And, then, after we have recognized who he is (*proskunew*), we are to add to that form of worship living in his service (*latreuw*).

True Worship

"God is spirit, and his worshipers must worship in spirit and in truth" (John 4:24). This verse is sometimes understood to mean that we must worship in the right frame of mind (the "spirit" aspect) and correctly (the "truth" aspect). Looking more closely, we can see that this is not what the text is saying. Here, *spirit* simply means non-physical as opposed to physical, as the woman was accustomed to. The Greek word used for truth is *alayth*, which means truly, or really, or genuinely. If *correctly* was the intended meaning, then *kalws*, which means rightly or correctly would have been used. Jesus is simply saying that when we worship God, we have to mean it.

Regarding this book's title—*Biblical Worship: Is It What You Think?*—The answer is a resounding *yes*; it is what you *think*. When you are thinking that God is awesome, you are worshiping *proskunew*. Biblical worship is also what you *act*. When you are acting in such a way that you are being spiritually "productive" you are worshiping *latreuw*.

Worshiping a non-physical God requires non-physical (spiritual) worship. But worship is also what you do. Presenting our bodies as living sacrifices (Romans 12:1,2) engages both the mind and the body. As our minds increase in faith, our bodies increase in action. Just as the high performance cycle in business suggests that motivation causes achievement which causes motivation, the same seems to be true in spiritual performance: Godly faith causes action which improves faith, and so on.

As long as our emphasis for worship is on a physical level, we are prone to error in how we carry out worship. Amos recorded some of God's most intense rebuking in the Bible, and it concerned how the Israelites were coming together to worship. Please read the entire book of Amos, but for now, let me put some of it in words for you:

> "I hate, I despise your religious feasts; I cannot stand your assemblies. Even though you bring me burnt offerings and grain offerings, I will not accept them. Though you bring choice fellowship offerings, I will have no regard for them. Away with the noise of your songs! I will not listen to the music of your harps. But let justice roll on like a river, righteousness like a never failing stream! Did you bring me sacrifices and offerings forty years in the desert, O house of Israel?" (Amos 5:21–25)

When we realize the spiritual nature of worship and that God, rather than demanding specific physical procedures for worship, has put in our hearts the ability to worship in spirit (non-physically), our worship will be both pleasing to him and fulfilling for us. As God reveals in Jeremiah 31:33, "This is the covenant I will make with the house of Israel after that time," declares the LORD. "I will put my law in their minds and write it on their hearts. I will be their God, and they will be my people."

Keeping the Spirit alive has two admonitions: 1) Don't quench the Spirit that is living in you, the temple of God; and 2) keep the spirit of restoration and continuous improvement alive by trying to practice biblical worship.

A Final Vision of Worship and Assembly

God is not pleased with those who want to build great buildings and make a name for themselves. Remember the tower of Babel? (Genesis 11:4). And he would rather us obey than to sacrifice (1 Samuel 15:22). All he requires of us is "to act justly and to love mercy and to walk humbly with our God" (Micah 6:8). Ultimately, how we attempt to walk humbly and live lives of worship to God is an internal matter of our own heart. Paul explained in Romans 14:4–8 that our relationship with God is a personal matter. And God, being our master, is able to make us stand.

As far as a final vision of worship, I could become utopic and borrow ideas from a distant galaxy depicted on some Star Trek episode. I could also be prescriptive in laying out how following generations of the church should worship and assemble. But in view of this study, anything I say would be adding to what God has established as a requirement. From everything this study has led me to believe, I think God is telling us that the fewer physical requirements we place on formal worship and assembly the better.

Well, sorry. As anticlimactic as it may appear, that's my vision: A system of worship and assembly that places as few requirements on people as possible. This vision also appears to shift the focus from asking, "What can I get out of worship?" to earnestly living out, "How can I help others?" That seems to be biblical worship.

This study has instilled in me the role I have as God's servant; that, as a priest in his service, I have a continual responsibility to be looking for ways to bring others to him and to encourage other priests to do the same. I am also finding that so many Christians (priests) are struggling to keep the faith, that it would be a full time job just ministering to them. And, of course, without other Christians also ministering to and challenging me, I would have trouble staying focused on the ministry God has given me.

Final Remarks

While in college I studied church history and since then have prepared and taught many Bible classes on the topic. It was not until reviewing church history references again that I noticed the surge of primary and secondary source publications during the 1950s concerning the early activities of Christians. I began to wonder whether these may have had more than casual correlation with the surge in church growth then and the decade immediately following. This interest in learning as much as possible about the early church may have been an outgrowth of their earnestness and loyalty to God.

Yeakley (Yeakley 1979) mentioned several Christian and congregational characteristics of growing churches in his statistical analysis of why churches grow. Yeakley also made several valid conclusions as to why the growth rate was declining. Though all of them are probably worth mentioning, he insightfully summarized the church's heart. "We have the manpower . . . brain power . . . financial power . . . communication power . . . gospel power. All that we lack is the will power" (Yeakley 1979, 122). Earlier in his summary, Yeakley advised preachers how to reverse the trend. Taking much of the blame away from the preacher, he then suggested that many congregations don't want to be challenged intellectually. He said, "They do not want to think" (Yeakley 1979, 121).

If we are going to keep the spirit alive, let's begin by revitalizing our hearts and minds. Peter said we should prepare our minds for action (1 Peter 1:13). It is fine with me if you disagree with every opinion in this study. But please think about the concepts presented and the challenges for conscientious word usage, communication with others, and continuous spiritual improvement. Let's reevaluate our concept of worship and consider how we should live lives of worship in view of God's amazing and wonderful grace.

After considering biblical worship and comparing it to the "old view" and what the intent has always been, we may find that our daily routine will not need to change much. Both views require living good moral lives in addition to assembling together. But having the knowledge to talk a certain manner of life is not enough. Motivation to continue walking in it is also necessary. Biblical worship may not call for a great revolution in practice, but it most assuredly calls for one in thinking. Wherever you are in your thinking about worship and fellowship and in your general walk with God, my prayer is that "He who began a good work in you will carry it on to completion until the day of Christ Jesus" (Philippians 1:6b).

Appendix A

Discussion/ Application Questions

There are purposely few enough questions after each section that you have no excuse but to answer all of them. Don't just do every other odd, etc., to see whether you have an understanding of the concepts. In fact, if you only read the study and don't give the questions considerable thought and time, you haven't participated in the study—you only listened to a lecture. Additionally, many of the points of this study are made only in the questions in an attempt to be less prescriptive in the study conclusions and implementations.

Part I: Background

Preface, rationale, overview, and approach of this study:

1. Philippians 3. What earthly credentials do you have that you consider rubbish? Which ones are you still holding on to?

2. How unsafe does it make you feel to study a lesson series developed by someone who is not a brother-hood-approved biblical scholar? Why?

3. What doors of opportunity has God opened for you? Which of them have you taken and which have you refused to accept?

4. Consider (and pick apart) this adage: "The best things in life are worth waiting for."

5. Consider how our immediate gratification society may be affecting our willingness and patience toward diligent Bible study.

6. Read 1 Kings 13. Paul may have had this story in mind when writing to the Galatians. Discuss the intensity Paul has when speaking in Galatians 1 about a conflicting message. Read all of Galatians and notice how upset Paul was that they believed false teachers. Think about the overall message of his letter and compare it to the worship issues we have today.

7. After understanding your personal responsibility to find out for yourself what God expects, how confi-dent/competent do you feel in this task? How are you going to improve your level of confidence/compe-tence? (Hint: 2 Corinthians 3:4–6, 2 Timothy 1:12)

Words Have Meaning:

1. Discuss the implicative differences between seman-tics and syntactics. (If you don't know what these words mean, look them up in a dictionary.)

2. Consider some words that people use inappropriately that result in miscommunication.
3. Think of the root meaning of a few words that you haven't considered before.
4. List some words in your vocabulary that probably aren't that "useful." Then find a friend willing help you eliminate them from your vocabulary.

   For items 5 through 8 research the origin and validity of the following mottos. Which of these are practiced at your congregation?
5. We are Christians only, but not the only Christians.
6. Speak where the Bible speaks and keep silent where the Bible is silent.
7. Call Bible things by Bible names.
8. In faith unity; in opinions liberty; in all things love.

Continuous Improvement:

1. A basic principle of quality is continuous improvement (the Japanese term is *kaizen*). Most businesses today must apply it or go out of business. How much emphasis do you place on continuous improvement in the personal and spiritual aspects of your life?
2. How open and ready for improvement is your congregation?
3. How could continuous improvement and humility work together in our lives?

4. Identify and list the fifteen or twenty primary processes of your church organization. (Processes may vary by congregation and could be anything from orienting a new member or preparing a new teacher to preparing the annual budget.)

5. Are those processes both effective and efficient? (Efficient is doing things right and effective is doing right things.) How could they be improved? Would everyone agree upon the processes you identified as being primary (why/why not)?

6. If your congregation has developed goals or a vision, what is being done to ensure that all members know what the plans are and where they fit in the realization of those plans? (If you don't have congregational plans, consider why not and determine whether they would help your congregation continuously improve.)

7. How could continuous improvement and biblical worship complement each other?

8. What would you say is the biggest impediment to congregational improvement?

Part II: Worship Versus Fellowship

Worship Word Study:

1. What does the New Testament call worship?

2. Discuss whether the biblical priority for worship is individual or corporate.

3. Where do congregations place emphasis for worship? Why would today's church get this confused?

4. At least one account of the early church tells how the Christians openly confessed wrongs and made verbal commitments to do right. How much is this practiced in the assemblies today? List a few barriers to this happening and envision the possible growth if we started doing this.

5. What can we do to change current practice toward a more biblical approach to worship?

6. Find at least three scriptural references that imply we should not only serve and suffer, but that we should do it with joy.

7. How could understanding the concept of worship on a broader sense make the assembly more meaningful to ourselves and others? (Romans 12, entire chapter)

8. How could allowing the awesome power of God to work in our daily lives, make the assembly more meaningful to us and others? (Hebrews 12, entire chapter)

Together Word Study:

1. Count the number of times "worship" is used in the same scriptural context as when the Christians came together for fellowship.

2. Which of the activities they did "together" were done in a central bona fide meeting place?

3. What activities did they do "together" that your church today may deem inappropriate or even wrong to do as a congregation that is "on congregational time"?

4. Think of ways to transform your "worship hour" into a place that recognizes the focus of being together—

fellowship—and that motivates each individual to serve—worship—God throughout the week.

5. Get a group of Christians to meet weekly at some publicly accessible location to pray and encourage each other. (Extra Credit: Do this with Christians from different congregations or even those believers not affiliated with your denomination.)

6. Assess the results of your experience from item 5 above. If the experience was positive, make changes to other assembly times to incorporate those practices. If it was a negative experience, assess why and make changes appropriately.

7. Discuss the advantages/disadvantages of organizing the congregation by age (youth group, college ministry, young adults, prime timers, etc.). What other ways might the organization be more effective?

Part III: Implications of Biblical Worship

Priority and Purpose of Assembly:

1. How are you going to explain to other congregational members your (possibly) new view of worship without making them angry at you or without coming across as self-righteous or even as a liberal?

2. How often do you meet with and encourage other Christians not counting the posted times of worship or Bible class at the building?

3. What would you think about a fellow church member who missed worship hour to visit someone who was shut in? (Luke 10:30f) What about an elder who

visited at a different congregation just to see how they functioned or to visit some former members?

4. If your congregational leaders suddenly decided to cancel Sunday evening services, what would your initial reaction be? What would you eventually put in its place?

5. What immediate changes must you now begin to make in the way you think about the worship service as it currently exists?

6. For each activity listed as a subheading in the chapter, what worship type (bow-down, service, etc.) would you consider that activity to be?

7. Recall the two greatest commands (Matthew 22:34c). Now think about the two prevailing kinds of worship (bow-down and service). What principles and worship priorities can you draw from this comparison (1 John 4:19–21)?

Disadvantages of Buildings as Places of Worship:

1. What would it be like to inherit something that was rather valuable, but that you really didn't want, or that cost more to maintain than you were willing to spend? What process would you use to determine the appropriate course of action?

2. Obtain a copy of your annual budget and calculate the percent of funds that go for benevolent or evangelistic purposes. (Caution: Think carefully about how much evangelizing is actually done from the pulpit before categorizing the pulpit minister's salary and benefits.)

3. How might the emphasis, topic, and duration of sermons change if the preacher was not standing behind a traditional pulpit in a traditional auditorium?

4. Consider the motives behind what you wear to the worship assembly. Would your attire change if you were meeting somewhere else to be together with Christians?

5. Review the ten disadvantages of buildings listed in the text. As some of them are stated in a rather formal manner, rewrite them so they better apply to your congregation and so you can better explain them to other church members not currently involved in this study.

6. List all the advantages of buildings you can think of and show that, overall, buildings are a necessary part of the church organization.

7. The alternative to item six above would be to either sell or bulldoze the building. What possibilities for good/bad advertising would this create? (It's okay to have fun with this question.)

Bureaucracy of the Modern Church Organization:

Be careful to answer these questions from the new view of biblical worship.

1. Consider how your congregation's Sunday school program is organized. What process is in place that ensures competent teachers? How do you relieve

teachers that prove themselves incompetent? (You do relieve incompetent teachers, don't you?)

2. If you operate using committees, do you use *Robert's Rules of Order* (conducting business with motions, seconds, votes, etc.) during meetings? How did you arrive at the decision to use that system?

3. Most congregations have a church phone number, or even better, a church office. Who runs the office? As the first line of contact representing the congregation to the outside world, who ensures it is operated by competent personnel?

4. Who is responsible for the budget: the congregation, ministers, elders, or deacons? Who should be? What should the budget be spent on? Who gets to spend church funds?

5. Should Christians "withhold" money from the worship hour collection to be used in individual "worship" throughout the week as we see the opportunity to do good? (Luke 10:30f; Ephesians 4:28)

6. What response would other congregations give if you sold your building or stopped using it as a primary location of worship? How would you react to their response?

7. Compare a typical Sunday morning Bible class to a meeting of the Areopagus (Mars Hill, Acts 17:16c). How different is your typical Bible class from a philosophical meeting?

Part IV Implementing Biblical Worship

Overcoming Disadvantages of Buildings:

1. What immediate changes must you now make in how you think about the formerly "non-worship" times of your life?
2. What would you now consider to be the primary function of the church building?
3. List several activities that could take place at the building location to improve the primary function of your congregation.
4. What is the difference between the allowed activities in the church building and those allowed activities away from the building location, say at summer church camp, or in a Christian's home? Justify all differences.
5. Make a verbal commitment to implement necessary changes in your lifestyle to make it one of perpetual worship to God.
6. How will this (possibly) new view of worship affect the way you evangelize your neighbors, community, and daily personal contacts?
7. How will this (possibly) new view of worship affect the way you think about your "free" time? (This is not the same question as #1 above.)
8. In light of Ephesians 5:16, what is free time?

Keeping the Spirit Alive:

1. What long-term adjustment in church culture can you begin anticipating and preparing for now?
2. How is your life of worship going to include service to other Christians?
3. What can you do, starting right now, to create a vision of worship to God that is visible and attractive to outsiders?
4. If this study has made an impact on your thinking, what is your responsibility to share it with others?
5. If by now you haven't read the remaining appendixes do that now. Consider how a better understanding both the word church (Appendix C) and church history (Appendix D) could help us appreciate where we are today.
6. Do you have a test of fellowship? If so, what is it? If not, should you have one?
7. Get a pen or pencil (now) and please send the author any comments, corrections, or questions about this book, biblical worship, or other topics this book presents. Thank you for your involvement with me in this study.

APPENDIX B

Non-Participant Observation of the Worship Hour

Just a little background about this appendix: It is actually a "qualitative non-participant observation" assignment of the qualitative methods course required as part of my leadership degree. I could have observed any group of people in any situation, but it was very intriguing for me to sit as a fly on the wall and observe what takes place in a worship assembly in which I normally would have been trying to concentrate on the service rather than the people and actions taking place during the service.

The lessons I learned from this observation not only helped me understand the benefit of qualitative or subjective research (as opposed to the quantitative or supposedly objective research I had been so accustomed to), but also taught me several lessons about how I viewed worship. The time frame of the observation was a Sunday morning in the fall of 1999. Nothing in the observation report is made up. It is a painstakingly accurate account of what I saw and heard during the data collection phase of my research. As you read this report think about your "worship hour" experiences and assess what you are doing during that time in light of the biblical definitions of worship. Here is the account of the observation:

Original Preface for the Worship Hour Observation

It has been said, "If you want to know what it's like to live in the water, don't ask a fish." A fish has nothing from which to reference its experiences. Accordingly, it may not be appropriate to ask a regular churchgoer what the worship hour is all about. Their perspective may be tainted by what their traditions have been telling them about the worship hour and not what it has become today.

The following non-fictional observation presents one such external perspective. The events recorded during the observation and expressed here are not meant to be taken negatively by any regular churchgoer. But it is my hope that by gaining insight into what we call the worship hour, true (genuine) worship to God may result, in the building, as well in our daily lives.

What's it all about? A Visitor's Perspective of Worship Hour

It's 10:00 A.M., time for the worship hour to begin, but people are still talking with each other and moving about. Teenagers—forty or fifty—are sitting together on the right about midway back. Four of the high school females are especially obvious. They are all the same height and have the same hair length but display four unique builds and clothing styles. Talking feverishly back and forth (as if there were no tomorrow), they are leaning their bodies into each other's personal space for a second or two then coiling back from the waist immediately. Older ladies are sitting in the middle sections closer to the back. There is *some* talking here, but no head turning, only an occasional body lean as if their gyro systems needed calibrating. It is unclear whether this procedure is to permit speaking with a lower voice, to foster better understanding, or to show respect and display an aura of maturity.

Families seem to form boundaries—or maybe couplings—between the other groups that have staked territories throughout the auditorium. Several individual adults around the auditorium, mostly men, are standing but bent over, talking quietly to others who have already been seated as if some sort of business negotiations were being conducted.

After looking around to ask permission from no particular person in the audience, a large man walks up about five steps onto a stage that juts out near the center. He stops behind a lectern and faces six or seven hundred men, women, and children. In a loud, deep voice, strengthened even more by a public address system, he speaks: "We'd like to welcome you to our service. For our first song, number One Hundred and forty-four. One, four, four." His words come out fast and well pronounced—not typical for a person from this area of the country. His large body size is reduced somewhat by the solid black dress suit and wide, dark, yet patterned tie, which leaves only a small amount of bright white shirt visible. His right arm rises and the first two fingers of his plump hand meet his thumb and freeze, signaling to the choir, "prepare to sing on my command." There is a pause. "Oh worship the King . . . ." There is no choir other than the audience, incorporating all ages, which begins to sing. There is neither a piano, organ, nor any other musical instrument in the building. Still, four parts of harmony blend together in choral fashion. ". . . all glorious above, and gratefully sing His wonderful love. Our Shield and Defender, the Ancient of days, pavilioned in splendor and girded with praise." The leader's voice, clear and strong, yet untrained, remains dominant throughout the song.

The worship hour has not yet begun for the four ladies mentioned previously. They are still uncoiling and recoiling, but in slower motion. Before the end of the song, one actually lifts a book from the pew in front of her. The song is over before she is able to open it and find one-four-four. Maybe it is not known by her that one-four-four is the proper page number to be on.

"Song before the opening prayer is number 800 . . . number 8-hundred." In the same choral manner, "What a Friend we have in Jesus" becomes the "song before the prayer." And, in the same manner, the four have not understood that worship hour has already begun. A gray-haired man and, apparently, his adult son walk briskly halfway down an outside aisle and are able to reach their final position unnoticed because of the singing. No one turns their head to see whether, or if, anything has changed outside of their focus on the songbook, and singing, and worshiping God, I presume.

The song is over and the leader sits down on a living room type chair upholstered with a not quite carpetbag patterned material. Another man, thinner and slower, takes the lectern wearing a gray suit and gray tie. The prayer is not rehearsed and not profound. Many blessings are asked for people, by name, who are sick or traveling out of town. The four are now leaning heads toward each other rather than turning them. One of them, the largest of the four, is using this opportunity to scan the crowd and the room, looking around in every direction and azimuth. She doesn't appear to be looking for anything or anyone, just looking and gazing. Many adult couples have their heads bent toward each other. An arm is around their spouse but resting on the pew back. As many women as men are displaying this gesture of protection or affection. Elsewhere, a mother clasps her hand over the mouth of a six-year-old boy. A different lady has finally found the time to clip her nails. Yes, clip her nails. The uniquely identifying staccato cheep, cheep, cheep heard several yards away (even up in the balcony) doesn't *seem* to be heard at all, even by those nearest to her. The prayer is not long enough to clip all her nails, but there will be more prayers. Never mind the thought of finding the nails weeks from now between the padded seat bottom and back. Never mind the fingernail mites that will live in style for months to come.

"Next song is number 453." The leader inserts a three-inch black-and-silver disk into his mouth and blows to retrieve a starting pitch. "Number 453." The audience/choir begins at his direction, "I was sinking deep in sin, far from the peaceful shore. Very deeply stained within. Sinking to rise no more . . . Love lifted me." The four are back to turning heads and leaning entire bodies into each other. One of them has an arm over the seat back around another. This domineering one looks loud even when her mouth is not moving. Her hair comes to just above her shoulder, as with the other three. It is mostly straight, with a slight bend to the side as it reaches its lower boundary—the shoulder. It would not be permitted to actually rest on the shoulder. To do so would be a symbol approaching pristine elegance, ruining the sassy freedom it now enjoys as their heads remain in constant motion.

In the opposite direction, a young mother with her infant, sitting only about twenty feet from a midway door, rises and begins to walk toward it. As she stops, rearranging her bundle to finagle the freedom of a shoulder or elbow to open the door, a thick, large, pink blanket drops to the floor and covers the six-inch space between her feet and the door. She pauses, noticing that something is different about her load. After looking around to see if she is disturbing anyone (don't worry, she isn't), she precariously lowers herself down to the auditorium floor and picks up the pink blanket, somehow . . . with her third hand. As she thrusts her body, and the young baby girl on her shoulder, back into the upright position, she leans into the door and disappears for the rest of the worship hour. "Looove lif-ted meee."

"As we prepare our minds to take the Lord's Supper, let's sing number 129." There is no repeat. There probably wasn't a need for one. "Amazing Grace how sweet the sound . . . that saved a wretch like me . . . ." The boy, whose mother smacked a hand over his mouth, is now waving a white bulletin either in an attempt to call the waiter over or to signal his surrender in the battle of trying to sit still for almost twenty minutes now. After a brief moment the mother grabs the flag and turns the son back around with the remaining arm and two eyes that were most definitely stronger than the arm.

Sixteen men, most wearing a tie, a couple wearing suit coats as well, have walked down the outside aisles, half on each side. They are standing in the side aisles except for the first two men in each line. These two presiders have taken positions behind small tables centered between the first row of pews and the first step of the stage. They are both standing "at ease" with arms folded in the front of their bodies rather than the back as in standard military formation style. Eventually, the song leader sits down and another presides over the lectern. With both elbows locked, his arms rest on the sides of the relatively low wooden apparatus. Its microphone is adjusted down, then up, then back to its exact origin. The arm returns to its previous position as well. "We are all here for only two reasons: 1) to feed our spiritual appetites . . . 2) to take the Lord's Supper . . . We feed our spiritual appetites by singing and praising God, and we gather now to take the Lord's Supper. Let us pray." The assistant presiders mechanically distribute plates of flat crackers as the well-choreographed lines pass by their respective tables before disbursing throughout the auditorium in service to the assembly. Oh, the four? In chorus girl fashion, they each have their left elbow on the seat back and their left hand over their left ear. What coordination. What style. What presence.

As the servers return to their positions, the speaker continues, "May I ask that you take the hand of the person next to you as we bow in prayer." Most do. Some don't. A few slide down as much as five feet to take the hand of their nearest neighbor. After the prayer, the same distribution procedure is repeated for a tray of small, half-filled cups containing just enough grape juice to wet ones lips, but not enough to wash through to the throat.

For the third time: "We are all rich. We have nice clothes, nice cars. We will probably eat out at nice restaurants—twice today, most likely. And then we give a little offering to God. Let's each reach in our pockets today. Grab that loose change and include it with your regular offering." Judging by the parking lot, hair and clothing styles, and physical breadth of the patrons, this prepared persuasive speech is probably applicable to at least forty percent of the congregation. By the same metrics, however, there is another thirty or forty percent that probably don't have a clue about what it's like to have ever eaten out twice in one day. They don't seem like the type to be worried about the kind of car they drive, but probably have more concern about how the next insurance premium is going to be paid on their ten or fifteen year old car. Nonetheless, the collection plates are scurried through the auditorium pew by pew.

The song leader returns to the lectern. "Would you please mark 652, number 652 . . . . Before the sermon, 381. As we are singing this song, please stand and the children may leave for children's worship." All stand. The singing begins and parents, mostly mothers, holding young babies, walk toward the back of the auditorium. The young children, now on their own, leave quickly, but aren't moving very fast. The song is over and without direction the assembly is seated. Some of the younger children, or guardians in their behalf, have decided it best to stay in the general assembly.

Another man, the first one to stand behind the lectern without a suit coat on, reads from the Bible (Romans 7:21 - 8:4) ". . . What a wretched man that I am. Who will rescue me from this body of death? Thanks be to God—Jesus Christ our Lord . . . There is therefore now no condemnation for those who are in Christ Jesus . . . ." He bounds off the stage and the small, young man of the hour, also without a coat on, steps up to fill the lectern's vacancy.

After a long few seconds of running his tongue across the internal recesses of his mouth, trying to remove the dryness, but also trying to look busy by rearranging his notes, Bible, and the microphone, which ends up in the same position as it was initially (again), he speaks. "We have some new members to introduce today: Mr. and Mrs. Jones [really] and their seven-month-old baby. Will you please stand? Are they here today? Are—are you here today? Oh, there you are. Welcome to the congregation, and it's a large congregation, so be sure and remind us to get to know you."

"My name is ___ ___ and I'm the visiting preacher to-day." It appears he is the youth minister regularly, and not usually the visiting preacher. He continues, "I always try to use current events when I'm teaching the kids. Today, since poison gases have been in our basement this week, I will be talking about poison gases . . . ." (I promise I am not making this up) He seems so unorganized—for a youth minister, much less a visiting preacher. Is this seem-ingly unorganized demeanor natural, or is it his way of presenting genuineness and sincerity? As a youth minister, maybe it's how he shows that he relates with the kids.

Four teenage boys, sitting in the same section but not contiguous to "the four," are reaching with long arms across two rows. It seems apparent that boys, and men in general, have a need for extending arms to their full length. Even the older adults, when they reposition, stand up, sit down, or move in any way, use their arms in some way, maybe to establish a presence. Maybe men's muscles just have a greater need to be stretched more often. Whatever the reason, male arm stretching is prevalent during this hour of worship.

A young lady, sitting immediately in front of "the four" moves her arms as little as possible as she puts a white sweater over the front of her body, covering both shoulders. The four are wearing completely different styles of clothing. All are long sleeved, but one, the largest of the equal-height musketeers, is wearing a thin, gray sweatshirt whose hood lies completely flat on her back. Next to her, the one with the darkest hair is wearing a white cotton blouse. The third displays a thin, knitted material as a collarless, sky blue pullover sweater. The fourth doesn't seem to belong with the other three, yet looks as if she wants to be considered a part of the other three. The third is now sitting with both elbows on the pew in front of her. Her face can be no more than four or five inches from bare neck of the young lady covering herself with the white sweater. I'm sure she feels the breath of the gang member behind her, but remains focused on the preacher, or lectern, or something in that general direction.

Some very young children are now *also* starting to fidget even though they are within an arm's reach of their parents.

Why are they still in the assembly? Did they not hear the announcement? Do they know something the others don't? What goes on at children's worship? Is the probability of their child making noise or causing them not to be able to hear the lesson that low? Or is the risk of leaving their child with someone just that high? For whatever reason their child had remained and is now tired of peace. The speaking interrupts, ". . . Lying starts small and grows . . . . If a problem is not recognized, how can it be addressed?" The four are all now sitting face forward, maybe for the first time since the worship hour began. Their heads are bowed and the one wearing blue has her arm on the seat back, resting, just barely, on the white blouse. Actually, the worship "hour" is over. Maybe they are tired of peace as well.

It's 11:00 o'clock. An aged lady, but not a widow, sitting in the back left section, steps over her husband and exits to the rear. She has white, white hair and is showing a bright red professional suit. She is also very tall for her age. Not only taller than her husband, but maybe something of an Amazon lady for her era. Even Amazon ladies can withhold it only so long.

"The reason it grows so quickly, is that we don't admit it's a problem . . . ." Now old and young alike begin to put away their active listening guides, which are printed on the back of the bulletin. Were they suddenly offended, or is it time for the lesson to be over? Whatever factors are to blame, it's time to put away the active listening guides. One man folds his in half and stores it in the left breast pocket of his suit coat. It will surely be reviewed at a later time this week or, at least, just before the jacket is taken to the cleaners. Paper is a wonderful invention. At the same time the active listening guides are being put away, the four have suddenly regained their enthusiasm. It seems that attendance cards are just the right size for passing information in written form, once your voice gets tired from talking all hour. This stroke of genius adds newfound energy and presence to their existence. It may be possible after all to make it through.

An old father or young grandfather carries out a three-year-old boy in his arms, walking from the front center section to the left midway door. It has been a popular door today. Seconds later, the Amazon lady returns, steps over her husband, and takes her place, just in time for the final words of the speaker before the invitation song where all those who want to take advantage of the Lord's invitation make themselves known by walking down the aisle and sitting on the front pew. Men's arms are moving again in full extension. "Don't think about which restaurant you are going to eat at today or what you are going to do after church is over, while we stand and sing this song."

"We have heard the joyful sound. Jesus Saves, Jesus Saves, Spread the tidings all around. Jesus Saves, Jesus Saves . . . ."

As the assembly sits down, again without being told, one couple walks out. Another man takes charge of the lectern and begins reading announcements. The four are just settling down and the one with the white blouse stands up and leaves through a back door of the auditorium. The larger one on the left with the hooded sweatshirt slides over to fill the gap as if a separation within the nucleus will cause some sort of atomic disaster. The father/grandfather brings his boy back to the front center section. The leader of the four, with the blue blouse, turns her head and entire body to the left, directly to the one with the hooded sweatshirt and begins to speak. The father/grandfather is a father because the boy is leaving again, this time with the mother, and the voice of the boy cries, "Daddy, Daddy."

Another song and a prayer become the last act [of worship] for this "worship hour" and it's over. Many must have heard a starting gun rather than an "amen" and are off. Several just stand there, maybe not quite sure that it's really over. Maybe they did listen to the preacher's closing remarks and after delaying their decision regarding where to eat, must only now determine an appropriate location for their dinner meal. Maybe they're tired after worshiping for a whole hour—more than a whole hour. Maybe they don't know they're just standing there.

Within five minutes of the amen, however, less than a third of the assembly remains. It is clear why they are still here. However engaged they were or not during the worship hour, they are engaged now. Smiles, laughs, genuine hugs, heartfelt handshakes, even a holy kiss. Fellowship. I'm not so sure about the "only two reasons for coming" talk. I'm not so sure why the other two-thirds were here, who were gone five minutes after the amen. I am sure these who remain have come to see family, and to them this was a fellowship dinner not only in the Lord's Supper, but in the reunion of brothers and sisters in the Lord's family. They will not leave hungry.

APPENDIX C

Multicontextual Nature of the Word Church

This appendix is a word study of *church* as it is used in different contexts in the New Testament, and the role elders may have had in the different contexts of church.

Where *church* is used in the New Testament, the Greek word *ekklesia* is most commonly used. From *Strong's Hebrew and Greek Lexicon* it is defined as follows:

G1577. *ekklesia* (ek klay see' ah); from a compound of G1537 and a derivative of G2564; a calling out, i.e. a popular meeting, especially a religious congregation (Jewish synagogue, or Christian community of members on earth or saints in heaven or both)—assembly, church.

(In 1 Peter 5:13, the word is even translated as "she" [who is in Babylon].)

Ekklesia is very broad in its scope and usage. It can represent at least seven different concepts:

1. *Non-religious assemblies* (Acts 19:32—a mob, Acts 19:39—a court of law).
2. Small *house churches* (1 Corinthians 16:19, Romans 16:4, Colossians 4:15, Philemon 1,2).
3. A *community of believers in general* (Acts 2:47; Acts 5:11, most references in the Corinthian letters).
4. The *Israelite nation* in the desert (Acts 7:38).
5. All the *Christians in one city* (Acts 8:1, Acts 11:22, Acts 11:26, 12:1, 12:5, 13:1, Acts 20:17, 1 Corinthians 1:2) Only the large cities are cited here to emphasize the unlikelihood of having only one congregation per city.
6. The entire *world's congregations* (Romans 16:16, 1 Corinthians 10:32, 1 Corinthians 11:16, 22, 1 Corinthians 12:28, 1 Corinthians 14:4, 1 Corinthians 15:9, Ephesians 1:22).
7. The *universal church*, including whatever portion of it that exists in the spiritual-only realm (Colossians 1:18, most references in the letter to the Ephesians, Hebrews 12:23).

The second and fifth concepts listed above (house churches and city churches) are most pertinent to this current study. Two specific questions have recently been asked. Were there smaller house churches within larger town or city churches? And, if so, were individual elderships established to shepherd over each smaller house church or over the more broad definition of church, the city church? Although not every single mention of *church* or *elder* is definitive, the references that are definitive point to an eldership that led city churches, not single house churches.

Acts 14:23 says that Paul (and his fellow missionaries) appointed elders in every church. But from the preceding verses, it appears that the churches in which they appointed elders were those in the cities of Derbe, Lystra, Iconium, and Antioch. In Acts 8–13 the word church (*ekklesia*) refers the Christians of an entire city. And beyond that, two of the city churches referred to were among the largest cities of the Roman Empire. Antioch was third largest, smaller only than Alexandria, Egypt, and Rome itself. We know that the population of Jerusalem was over 600,000 because during the fall of Jerusalem more than that number were killed by the Roman Army (PC Bible Atlas). Thousands more were taken away into captivity. During the period when Acts was written, it has been estimated that as many as 20,000 Christians lived in Jerusalem. It is not likely that only one congregation, as we know it, existed in Jerusalem. No mention is made of the "elders from the Main Street Church," only elders of the city. "And when they had come to Jerusalem, they were received by the church and the apostles and the elders" (Acts 15:4, NKJV).

Yes, it is possible that the elders could have been a collection of elders from all the "elderships" within the different congregations, or mini-churches, of the city. (Recall the references to city churches listed above where each city is hundreds of thousands in size—Jerusalem, Antioch, Ephesus, and Corinth.) But it requires less inference to believe there was one eldership for the entire city. Besides, if there were elders in each different congregation (mini-church) of the city, then Acts 15 authorizes a hierarchical organization like the Catholic Church practices. I'm sure that's not what those opposing the idea of city elders would have us believe. In fact, generally, hierarchical leadership is explicitly condemned by those opposing meeting outside of the building.

(Acts 16:4 sheds a very interesting light on the topic. Some church "experts" usually dismiss Jerusalem as a church headquarters stating that the church was in its infancy and the apostles were interim leaders until the church was better established. But Acts 16:4 says the apostles *and* the elders (city elders) were the ones who determined decrees to be adhered by other churches.)

To summarize, the word *church* has a broad meaning, so when Acts 14:23 says that elders were appointed in every church, it is easy to interpret church as city church (multiple house-churches). But when Titus 1:5 says to appoint elders in every city, city cannot have a broad meaning. In order to keep the Bible from contradicting itself (which it can't—integrity of the Word is essential to our faith) only two possible answers are permitted, both of which could be true. Most likely is that elders were probably appointed for each city, not each mini-church. Another possibility is that God left that aspect of organizational leadership up to man to decide. In other words, Paul did what was best for the situation he was in, and told Titus to do something different because Titus was in a different situation and God didn't care which way it was done.

Here is another example showing multiple mini-churches (house churches) in one city with one eldership. Aquila and Priscilla had a church that met in their house. But they lived in Ephesus that had *city* elders: "The churches in the province of Asia send you greetings. Aquila and Priscilla greet you warmly in the Lord, and so does the church that meets at their house" (1 Corinthians 16:19).

Several other house churches are also mentioned in the Bible:

House church of Priscilla and Aquila

"Greet Priscilla and Aquila, my fellow workers in Christ Jesus. They risked their lives for me. Not only I but all the churches of the Gentiles are grateful to them. Greet also the church that meets at their house. Greet my dear friend Epenetus, who was the first convert to Christ in the province of Asia." *(Romans 16:3–5)*

House church of Nymphas

"Greet the brethren who are in Laodicea, and Nymphas and the church that is in his house." (Colossians 4:15, NKJV)

House church of Philemon

"Paul, a prisoner of Christ Jesus, and Timothy our brother, To Philemon our beloved friend and fellow laborer, to the beloved Apphia, Archippus our fellow soldier, and to the church in your house . . . ." (Philemon 1:1–2, NKJV)

In Rome

Romans 16:15 mentions all the saints with them as if they formed a mini-church within the church at Rome.

Of Lydia

Lydia may have had a church that met in her house. "After Paul and Silas came out of the prison, they went to Lydia's house where they met with the brothers and encouraged them. Then they left" (Acts 16:40). "One of those listening was a woman named Lydia, a dealer in purple cloth from the city of Thyatira, who was a worshiper of God. The Lord opened her heart to respond to Paul's message. When she and the members of her household were baptized, she invited us to her home. 'If you consider me a believer in the Lord,' she said, 'come and stay at my house.' And she persuaded us" (Acts 16:14, 15).

Several other households are mentioned that, in my opinion, are referring to house churches, but, since they are not explicitly identified as such, they have been omitted from this list.

Conclusion

It is not my suggestion to hold our breath until the several congregations of every city have been consolidated under one city eldership. Refer to the chapter on bureaucracy of the modern church organization to understand the possible complications of doing so. But certainly New Testament precedence and direction of smaller home Bible studies or mini-churches on Sundays is closer to what actually occurred in the first century than our current tradition of "bigger is better."

One possible outcome of this study, when considering the discussion on the disadvantages of church buildings, may be, that if there were no buildings, there may be city elders rather than congregational elders. Imagine the unity of *that* situation.

Appendix D

Etiology of Current Building/ Worship Practice

I t is apparent that even under the old law, the Jews congregated to sing, listen to the reading of the Law, and pray. Mark 14:49 depicts Jesus meeting in the temple courts every day. During the time of Christ, and after his death, there were meetings in synagogues, the local "church buildings." Read Luke 4:21 where Jesus was in a synagogue reading Scripture. When Paul went on his missionary journeys, his typical routine was to meet in the synagogue with the Jews until they either kicked him out or he saw that he wasn't making any more progress there. But, except possibly for some the Jewish Christians, the church didn't meet in the synagogues.

Christians did meet in the temple courts, as we have already discussed in this text. But primarily, it seems that they met in the homes of Christians, with Lydia (meeting by the river) being a notable exception (Acts 16:13f). We have also previously discussed what they did when they were together. And by looking at several passages, it is possible to find what are sometimes referred to today as the five acts of worship. One of the most notorious proof texts for meeting formally on Sunday and taking the Lord's Supper is Acts 20:7. Paul's letters to the Corinthians (especially 1 Corinthians 11–14) verify meeting together in a semblance of what most Christians today consider a worship service.

To ascertain what was really happening we need to look at the contexts carefully. For example, it is now understood that breaking bread referred to an entire fellowship meal that included bread and wine (Storm 2003). Remember our discussion in chapter two about the meaning of words. If we want to copy the early church, we can't do it by trying to mimic what they did. There is not time to discuss movements here, but we can only have a movement like the first-century church if we listen to the same message that they did. (After reading Galatians and Corinthians, however, I'm not sure whether I want to have a church like they had in the first century.)

In the fourth century, after Constantine began to build church buildings (Ferguson 1971) and the church began to evolve toward an institution, assembly activities probably also began to fossilize. Bishops led the church using an organizational hierarchy. By the Nicaean Council of 325 A.D., Constantine called himself the "bishop of bishops" (Mattox 1961, 128). During the fourth and fifth centuries the bishops grew in power and hierarchy. The power of Christ as prophet, priest, and king began to be transferred to the bishops and church organization (Mattox 1971, 160).

By the twelfth and thirteenth centuries, the papal system had total power and control over the citizenry and civil government. The priests, or clergy, "knew everything" and everyone else, the common people or laity, "knew nothing." In fact, few of the laity could even read. This is not how the church began in the first century where, for example, the Bereans went home and searched the Scriptures to see if the preacher was correct (Acts 17:11).

Also by this time, the fellowship meal had become a solemn ritual where the priest placed a wafer in the mouth of the laity, and at times, the priest alone drank the cup. The service, mass, or liturgy, became a time where the people only received and didn't fellowship by taking and receiving (except for the church tax that was levied on everyone). With one-way communication and a spiritually-elevated priest, it was only natural that pews all face the same direction—forward and up to the priest, who stood on a stage or pedestal. Literal partition fences separated clergy from laity (many Catholic and denominational buildings have these fences today). The large pipe organ played the music so the people didn't even have to sing anymore. Worship had become a concept that was completely one way and ritualistic.

From about 1500–1800 A.D., reformists (e.g., Martin Luther) protested the power and some of the flawed ritualistic procedures of the Catholic Church with some success and with no, or little, intention of abandoning the church. Yet others (e.g., John Smyth) during this time openly protested the Catholic system and began to divide over and over into different denominations (Mattox 1961, 308).

From the beginning of the nineteenth century on, some saw that continuous division was not good and tried to unite on the belief that there is only one Christ and one church

(Ephesians 4:1c). So, in doctrines such as original sin, infant baptism, or transubstantiation, the Bible was used as the sole authority and, in many cases, the correct biblical doctrines were being restored. But in practice not much was changing. The preacher, although not considered a priest, still stood up on a pedestal with the members sitting in pews facing in the same direction. The Lord's Supper was still only a tiny piece of unleavened bread with a sip of grape juice or wine. Worship service was generally still considered only what went on at the building rather than what went on in the heart. Institutions die hard.

Part of the reason for not changing these practices may have been that the current secular culture developed to incorporate church culture. Let's briefly review how societal culture and church culture parallel each other. Being a military veteran, I will use the military culture also in this analogy, looking at how battles have been fought over the last several decades with how churches have operated during corresponding time periods. (I apologize for the oversimplification of this appendix, but I only want to give the idea of how we got where we are. Being only a tertiary source on this topic I cannot permit myself to get into too much detail.)

The church movement, or denomination, we now know as the "Disciples of Christ" began in the early 1800s, as several independent ministers and parishioners began to feel that their current denominational associations and organizations were mandating too much in the way of creeds and doctrines. By the 1830s and 1840s many congregations began to claim autonomy and secede from the larger unions of the Presbyterian, Methodist, or Baptist organizations.

The southern states of the Union also wanted freedom from the Federation and so attempted to secede. The Civil War ensued. Armies lined up opposing each other and fought each other open column to open column. Nothing deceitful about their methods. Men with honor fought honorably for what they believed. Accordingly, in the church, open debates were common during this time. Men spoke openly about what they believed, and they stood firmly on their ground.

By the time WW II had ended, world culture had further developed and technology had become a way of life. Scientific process was widespread. In battle, specific and technical procedures ensured the greatest statistical "probability" of success. Pilots had checklists for starting engines, taking off, bomb runs, etc. The Church of Christ that had earlier divided over issues such as musical instruments in "worship" and the appropriateness of funding denominationally combined missionary societies, now also employed specific procedures and scientific-sounding methods (e.g., five acts of worship, five steps of conversion, specific times and formats for "worship"). Because of some of these dogmatic procedures and thought processes, the church effectively split again in the 1950s along institutional and non-institutional persuasions.

The Cold War brought fear (as much fear of "commies" as of the "nukes") while the socialist/communist movement brought rebellion and the false promise of simultaneous freedom and equality (Rokeach 1973) concealed in a cloak of decency and tolerance. Although the Church of Christ became the fastest growing religious movement in the 1960s (Yeakley 1979), due to cultural revolution in the same decade, the methodological principles that made the movement strong eventually also began to disintegrate it. By the early 1980s, the growth rate of the movement was negative (primarily because tactics didn't change with the times).

In the mid 1980s community churches began to spring up in every suburb—not necessarily Baptist, or Presbyterian, or any other denomination. Honestly, they were very similar to those congregations of the early days of the Restoration Movement, not wanting to be a part of any denominational squabbling and not wanting to take orders from any synod or headquarters. Some of the more conservative groups began to "circle the wagons" to protect what was left of their heritage and "correctness."

Today, the military has a "new" war-fighting strategy: Asymmetric Attack. It's what the terrorists have already learned: fight only where you have a distinct advantage, where few can overcome many and weak can overpower strong. Control the tactics and locations of your battle and you will win. This is a biblical concept. How can we apply it to the practice of biblical worship and fellowship?

In many areas, the church as we know it is dying. To revive the movement we must get back in touch with the man who started it, Jesus, the Christ. Revival will not occur by resurrecting practices and procedures from thirty or fifty years ago. We would not think of trying to transplant an American church to a foreign country with all our traditions and expect it to survive, because we know that foreign cultures need to learn about Christ and then create their own church culture. Why do we think that anything less is possible with subsequent generations of churches in America? If anyone doesn't think our children are living in a different culture than we are, they are more asleep than Mr. VanWinkle. The church in America will survive only if we first give our children Christ and then let them adapt the church as they know best.

Bibliography

Covey, Stephen. 1989. *The Seven Habits of Highly Effective People: Restoring the Character Ethic*, New York: Simon and Schuster.

Ferguson, Everett. 1971. *Early Christians Speak*, Austin, Texas: Sweet Publishing Company

Hall, Richard. 1999. *Organizations: Structures, Processes, and Outcomes,* 7th ed., Upper Saddle River, New Jersey: Prentice Hall.

Hawley, Monroe. 1976. *Redigging the Wells: Seeking Undenominational Christianity*, Abilene, Texas: Quality Publications.

Hawley, Monroe. 1981. *Searching for a Better Way*, Abilene, Texas: Quality Publications.

Hawley, Monroe. 1985. *The Focus of Our Faith*, Nashville, Tennessee: 20th Century Christian Foundation.

Hawley, Monroe. 1992. *Is Christ Divided: A Study of Sectarianism*, West Monroe, Louisiana: Howard Publishing Co.

Howard, D. R. 1990. *Crisis in Education*, Green Forest, Arkansas: New Leaf Press.

Lynn, Mac. 1997. *Churches of Christ in the United States*, Nashville, Tennessee: 21st Century Christian.

Mattox, F. W. 1961. *The Eternal Kingdom*, Delight, Arkansas: Gospel Light Publishing Company.

Postman, Neil. 1992. *Technopoly: The Surrender of Culture to Technology*, New York: Knopf.

Rokeach, Milton. 1973. *The Nature of Human Values*. New York: The Free Press.

Storm, Melvin. April 16, 2003. E-mail correspondence with Bible Department Chair at Rochester College, Rochester Hills, MI.

Yeakley, Flavel. 1979. *Why Churches Grow*, 3rd ed., Broken Arrow, Oklahoma: Christian Communications, Inc.

Please e-mail the author with
comments and questions at:
rob.byrd@york.edu

To order additional copies of

BIBLICAL
WORSHIP

Have your credit card ready and call

Toll free: (800) 950-YORK (9675) M–F 9–5 CST

Order online at www.york.edu/biblicalworship

or send request with proper payment* to

York College Bookstore
Attn: Biblical Worship
1125 East 8th St.
York, Nebraska 68467

Price Schedule

1 book	$14.00 plus $3.00 S&H
2–5 books	$13.00 each plus $5.00 S&H
6–10 books	$12.00 each plus $7.50 S&H
11 or more books	$12.00 each plus free S&H

*Nebraska residents include 6% tax or tax exempt number